THREE LIONS AND A KITTEN

Three lions and a kitten
A short story about a long love

Dedications and special thanks

I would like to dedicate this book to my dearest father whom without, this adventure never would have been possible. My father is a hero, a legend and a man of patience and I couldn't of asked for a better travel companion throughout the years. I would also like to thank my father on behalf of Germany for single-handedly increasing their apple wine consumption 2006. Real boost for the economy dad. Special thanks to my mother, the patience of a saint, who tirelessly listened to my elaborate travel plans without poking fun and who put up with me and dad missing various important family events. I would like to thank Chris for saving my life, not only in Russia but in general. Thanks to all the other usual suspects who's travelled beside me the past decades, there's too many to mention but most of you are featured in this book one way or another. Don't worry, I've changed your names so your family don't have to ring you up and ask about what you did in Zagreb... I love you like brothers and sisters. It sounds like a cliché but I do. I know that we will be bonded forever through the football and that's a wonderful thing.

Thank you to my Pete, who has supported me and pushed me when I felt as if this novel wasn't such a good idea, you are a daily inspiration to me and without you, I probably wouldn't have had the guts to publish a book.

To my best buddy and brother Jez, thanks for always being there and for looking after mum when me and dad were less present.

To my children Billy and Emmy. Thanks for being so encouraging and for not telling me that its embarrassing that I'm publishing a book. You both have qualities and traits I admire deeply. Keep being you.

Finally I would like to dedicate this book to Deb Matthews, my dear mother in law who sadly passed away before I published this book. She lived her life to the full, beautiful and unapologetic and I intend to do the same. She taught me so much in such a short time and I will forever be grateful for her impact and for her wonderful son whom I intend to love for the rest of my life.

This novel is for all of you. Thank you.

Prologue

"What are you wearing?" My mate looked at me in absolute disbelief as I showed up wearing an England top to my Swedish high school the day after England played Sweden in the World Cup 2002. I just shrugged my shoulders.

"What does it matter?"

It did matter to several of the lads in school, though. As soon as they spotted me walking through the sea of students in the corridor in my red top they started taunting me, but it was mostly lovingly. They had known me for 3 years throughout high school and was very aware of my football preferences by now. It was a constant topic of conversations and sometimes they took it too far and we ended up wrestling on the ground over it. I was the epitome of a tomboy. Not very feminine, not very delicate, and with a mouth that got me into trouble daily. I had friends but never really fitted in. They were talking about boys and make up and I was talking about Michael Owen and the group of death. Their locker had pictures of pop bands and mine had a picture of Paul Scholes. I was not bothered about not fitting in, though. I think it sort of became my niche to be the odd one out. Everyone knew me and I was always up for a laugh and a bit of wrestling. One time they bet me I couldn't fit into my locker. I laughed and climbed in quite comfortably.

"See, I'm in, the laughs on you!"

It wasn't on them, they locked the locker and told me I couldn't come out until I admitted Sweden are better than England and that I was dumb. Needless to say I said no such thing, and the janitor eventually came and let me out, slightly puzzled as to why I was in there.

A few weeks later we were graduating from high school. We had a trip booked in the afternoon and of course it collided with England playing Argentina. I rushed back from the morning ceremony at school to watch the first half before the coach was leaving for the graduation day trip.

After a goalless first half I stood up and went to go put my heels on ready to leave. There was just a few minutes left of the half. Just as I had got them on I hear my dad shouting at the top of his lungs:

"Penaltyyyyyyy, Az, it's a penalty to England!" I ran up the stairs and into the lounge - I technically had to leave now to catch the coach but I had to see this.

Beckham was taking it. Beckham who 4 years earlier in the World Cup 1998 had been sent off against Argentina and we lost. My heart was pounding in my chest. My dad was stood up leaning against the armchair. My brother had covered his eyes. Beckham stepped up and took the shot, I watched as it slowly went past Cavallero and hit the back of the net.

We all exploded in a pile of joy and it wasn't until we got back up that I realised I had to rush. Mum was muttering about the fact that dad had jumped so high after the goal he had knocked a hole in the paper ceiling.

I grabbed the little radio so I could listen to the game on the coach before making my way out the front door. It's not easy running in heels and when I got to school the coach was waiting for me. I entered it red faced and victorious., " Its fucking 1-0 to England did you see it?" I loudly exclaimed to my mate who had very little interest in football and who seemed annoyed that I was late. She said nothing for the rest of the coach journey which was no problem for me. I was engrossed in my radio and had no time to small talk.

England won 1-0 after a very tactical second half by us. We had a good time at the venue, the usual shenanigans when 15 year olds get together to graduate from high school I guess. I fell asleep on the coach home and was abruptly awoken by my mate howling across the coach.

"Az, Az look out the window, your family are dancing on the balcony."

As the coach passed my house I looked at my dad on the balcony, music blasting, lights flashing and him topless waving an England flag. My friend patted my back and laughed.

"You're all equally crazy aren't you? I swear someone will write a book about you one day..."

Chapter 1
You're not from here are you?

My hands were shaking as I attempted to balance two pints in my small hands through a packed pub full of men bouncing up and down. The smell of sweat and beer were thick in the air and my arms were soaked in what I could only assume was a mix of both. I tried squinting to spot my dad's familiar face in the crowd. He was tall, slim and looked a lot like Flanders from *The Simpsons*. Together we did not look like the stereotypical picture of an England fan that the media loved painting to the public. That's because we weren't. My dad was a quiet reserved man in his mid-40's and I was a 19 year old girl. What's even weirder was that we were from Sweden.

OK, I'm going to say that again just so that it properly sink in. We were from Sweden. I sometimes wish we weren't. It would of saved us and me so many conversations and a sense of constantly having to prove that we were genuine. The Brits, footballs fans in particular, are very, very patriotic. To try and explain to them that you don't follow your country's football, but another's was a task that wore me down throughout the years and made me question my own sanity at one point. I was met with acceptance most of the times however and I came to form some friendships through football that followed me into adult life and became vital. It sounds like a cliché but there is such a thing as a football family, a sense of belonging for which my lost teenage heart had searched for a long time.

Why England though? Is there a reason? Wouldn't it have saved me so much money to just support and follow my own country?

Of course it would but life isn't always straight forward. It kind of does what it wants in terms of the journey it will take you on. I am forever grateful for mine. I'm convinced that it both saved and shaped my life. It started in 1998.

The 1998 World Cup in France; what a tournament, and in my case, a life changing few months.

I had always been into football for as long as I can remember. My dad was the coach of my brother's football team and we spent every weekend going to watch them play. My dad lived for football and up until today I'm yet to come across someone that appreciates the sport more than him.

He was a fanatic and he drilled into my head very early that football was everything. My dad had a soft spot for English football and so did my brother who's big role model in life was Alan Shearer.

I hadn't started supporting anyone as such at this stage. I was a 12 year old girl and most of my friends had no interest in football at all. I followed all the games though with great interest and hoped for Sweden to do well. Something strange happened that summer however, my dad called me into the lounge before England was playing Tunisia. It was a warm summer afternoon and our lounge was muggy. Dad was sat in his chair topless. He was often topless in all fairness; weather played a very small role in his lack of clothing.

The British were lined up on the TV screen during the national anthem. The camera was sweeping over the faces of Shearer, Sheringham, Seaman and company and onto the sea of England fans singing along proudly. My dad turned to me and held his arm out.

"Look at this, I've got goosebumps."

He went on to tell me that these are the real football players. "The heart of proper football is England, they're lions and their fans are the real ones, the passionate ones."

I sat down to watch and I guess you could put it in a really simple way. I fell head over heel in love. My dad's constant speeches about the pride of these lions mixed with the passionate football got me. I remember thinking to myself that this is it. England is the team I want to follow. I suppose patriotism and things like being a traitor didn't really reason with me at that point. It's quite simple when you're a kid really, you see something you like and you take it. I saw England. I saw the battle on the pitch, the fans on the stands and Shearer banging in goals and I felt a sense of homecoming. This was something I wanted to be a part of.

I didn't quite grasp it then, but that game changed my entire life. It started something that was to become so big it defined my whole life. This little 12 year old girl who weeks later cried herself to sleep when England lost to Argentina had no idea what she had started. My dad sat on the side of me and my brothers bed as we were sobbing into our pillows and he said something that's been ringing in my head ever since, every time we've lost a game.

"Kids there will come a day tomorrow again, when the grass will still be green, the sky blue and the house will still be here. Things will go on."

I have thought about that many, many times since then. About the innocence of it and how it came to represent the start of absolutely everything. I cried myself to sleep that night. Football had proven itself to be really unfair. I didn't know it then but my story started there, 30th of June 1998 after England lost to Argentina on penalties and my dad delivered what was to become his most famous speech.

Now it was 7 years later and me and my dad were in Denmark at our first away game.
We had took the bus there and not even booked a hotel.

"We will stay in pubs till they close and then sleep on a bench until the coach goes back in the morning," my dad declared to my mum over dinner a few months earlier. Mum was apprehensive. Was this violent world of football really the place for a 19 year old girl who already had a tendency of causing trouble?

I was stubborn though. I had nagged at dad for years to join England fans and start going to games.
He had finally given in and we were now in a pub in Copenhagen about to meet up with the rest of the football fans. I was kind of nervous - what if they wouldn't accept us? All these years watching England play on TV and falling deeper and deeper in love with everything they were had lead up to this very moment. This shaky walk across a crowded room with two pints that now were half

empty due to the inevitable spillage.

I could finally spot my dad through the crowd of big broad shoulders. He was stood at a table listening intensely to a big fella with the union jack across his back. He looked happy. Like he belonged there in a strange way. When he saw me coming he made a big sweeping gesture.

"Az, this is Ricky. He was just telling me about Italy 90, come listen to this."

Ricky turned to me and held his big tattooed hand out "Pleasure, Az. Now get that beer down ya, you've got a 90 min game of dreadful football to suffer through" He laughed a big deep laugh at his own joke, and pat me on the back before returning to Italy 90.

I smiled to myself. We were finally home.

Chapter 2
Rosie McGee's

I think that whole afternoon was everything I had dreamt of when watching England on TV. Not only had people accepted us but they had welcomed us. We got a mention over the microphone and before I knew it I was up there singing karaoke with a few of them. It was a great atmosphere and I thought to myself: imagine not being part of this? Imagine not liking football and never experience that thrill. My head was filled with euphoria that day. When we joined England fans we also became part of their forum and today was about meeting all them faces we had come across the past few months leading up to this trip. I think I lost count of all the different people and handshakes after a while.

" Az, guess who I am?" I turned around and a large lad with a bald head was stood there grinning.
I had met so many people I had no clue.

" It's me, Denny!" He picked me up and spun me around. Denny was a notorious face on the forum and a keen wind up merchant. We had talked quite a lot on the forum but never met, and it was crazy seeing them all now, like characters from a book coming to life. We went on to become good friends after that and even though I don't see him at games anymore I know for a fact that should I see him tomorrow we would pick up where we left. Football works like that; it's not the usual friendships. You go months of not seeing each other just to run into each other in some backstreet bar in a European country and you're best mates again. You share beds, laughs, brawls and memories and the second you part to go home you know that it can be months before next time but it doesn't matter. You're sort of bonded for life.

It was time to head over to the game. Denny and the rest told me they're taking a taxi but my money conscious dad declared that we were walking. It was "only" 30 mins. 30 mins is a lot when you've drank all afternoon and been dropped on the floor at least three times. My dad is a man of nostalgia and on our forever walk to Parken Stadium he got lost in it. I was starting to regret those last pints as my bladder were now telling me we needed the toilet. As dad were going on about English football in the 70's I was dreaming of dirty stadium toilets. When we got there the queue was fairly short because it was still early. Dad liked to be at the stadium early to soak up the atmosphere of what I presumed would be empty seats at this time. I ran to the toilet and came to the conclusion that being female at football had its perks; the ladies toilet was empty except for a large woman in a tight England top that was doing its best to keep her blossoming chest inside of it.

"Aren't you a little cute one?" she laughed at me whilst meeting my eyes in the mirror. "You've not come alone have you? This world is no place for a young girl alone."

I reassured her that I had plenty of company. That comment stuck with me though, and years later whenever I found myself alone in a foreign country I would hear her voice echo in my head in her broad Manchester accent. It's funny how some people who only flash by in your life still manage to leave an impression. She was brutally mistaken though. This world was the right place for me. It was a home away from home that I would come to rely on in the next decade to come.

I returned to our seats and my dad was muttering that I had been gone a long time. The game was about to start and I was excited. When we stood up to sing the national anthem I never really paid any thoughts to the fact I was singing another country's anthem like it was my own. I felt like I belonged there.

We don't need a long account of that game now do we? David James had an absolute nightmare and we lost 4-1 after Denmark scored 3 goals in 7 minutes. It was humiliating and I was disappointed. The walk back from the stadium seemed so much longer now. Dad was sulking and getting angry with all the Danish

youths that were getting in his way as he was power walking d‹
Copenhagen's busy streets. I remember being that thirsty all I could
think of was Smirnoff ice. We hadn't eaten all day and my dad
started to flag a bit. He told me to continue to the pub whilst he
queued up to get some food. I was slightly hesitant leaving him
alone but continued. This was back in the era where my dad refused
to have a mobile phone so if you lost him you lost him for real. As I
got into the pub after a walk that felt like two days in the desert
everyone was already there. I was expecting a bit of a bad
atmosphere seeing as we had lost but everyone was cheery. I downed
my sought after Smirnoff ice and made my way over to a group of
now familiar faces.

"Come here chin up, its only football. The real fun starts here," one
of the lads laughed as he picked me up and put me back down. I
never really got used to that even after years of going to football. To
me if we lost I would sulk endlessly. Today was however a silly
friendly, and who cared about that? Not us. We had the qualifiers to
look forward to in October and me and dad had tickets for both
games. I felt like my life started here. We had gotten over the first
hurdle and been somewhat accepted amongst the fans and what was
ahead of us now was to become an endless adventure.
As my dad returned to the pub I was on my mates shoulders singing
and he soon joined in. I don't know what we were singing about but
it didn't matter. This was the life.

After the pub closed we went to a convenience store to get some
water and snacks for the coach.
It was 5am something, the streets of Copenhagen were empty and
the morning sun was dancing on the cobbled streets. The coach
station wasn't a coach station as such but merely a bench on the side
of the road. We sat down and dad started fidgeting with his water
bottle to get it to open. I curled up on the other side of the bench and
wrapped my flag around me like a quilt. I could hear the sound of
the early morning sweeping machines cleaning up the streets in the
background as I closed my eyes to rest.

" You know what, I think this is just the beginning," I said to dad as
I drifted off on the park bench.

Chapter 3
Manchester – Dad's umbrella rampage

It didn't take long after we got back from Denmark for me to start nagging at my dad about going over to Manchester for our final qualifier games against Austria and Poland.

"We can't go to every single game Aza, it's not feasible in the long run," he said in a tired voice as we sat down to eat dinner. Mum was absolutely agreeing with this - she wasn't a keen supporter of my elaborate plans to attend any game I could. I had savings though, and a good paying job; I saw absolutely no reason as to why I wouldn't try and go to as many games as possible. Eventually, I convinced dad. There was never really any doubt about it. Dad just liked to pretend that he was objecting when in reality, this was his dream as well. It didn't take long before we had booked a hotel for a week and flights to Manchester. I was finally about to visit the country that I was hoping would be my home one day.
There was just one small little detail: dad and I had never been on a plane before in our lives. We had always taken ridiculous measures as to avoid it, but we couldn't anymore.
I think I dreamt about our plane bursting into flames at least three nights leading up to our trip.

" I feel a bit sick if I'm honest," I whispered to dad as the small plane prepared for take-off. It was one of the little planes with a propeller and two seats on each side of the aisle. I had only seen planes on TV, and they did not look like this. I had my portable CD player in a firm grip (yes this was that long ago that portable CD players were a thing, imagine!) and when we took off, I got so sweaty that it slid out of my hands and down on the floor. Dad glanced at me but said nothing. It was only a short 30 min flight between my hometown and Copenhagen. We then had to take another longer flight from Copenhagen to Manchester. If you've ever come in from Sweden to Copenhagen airport you know how sweaty that landing is, as you're coming in and landing over water. For a frequent flyer this would not be alarming, but for me, who had never flown before, it felt like Armageddon. I was silently wondering what mum would say in my eulogy - but before I got to the good parts we had landed.

The rest of the trip went fairly smoothly; a bus followed the second plane, and dad had his map out, much to my embarrassment. We were on a bus, so I really didn't see the need for a fold out map, but the man lived to be prepared. He knew we had to walk for a few blocks once we got off the bus and God forbid he hadn't already sussed out the fastest route.

"I don't think this is a hotel dad!" I exclaimed as we had stopped in front of a worn-down building. It was dark outside, and it looked a bit like the sort of accommodation Norman Bates would get murdery in. Dad laughed and continued walking towards the door of murder city. I followed him reluctantly. The inside was no better and that's an understatement. The beds, if you can call them that, had no quilts, just some sort of blanket with fag burns on.

"It kinda feels like I needed a jab before sleeping in here," I said jokingly as we prepared for bed.
" At least we are in England," Dad replied, with his never ending positivity.
He was right. The only accommodation that could of possibly been worse would have been Fritzl's basement, but at least we were here. The adventure was about to begin and as I drifted off that night I had no idea the following days would involve swinging umbrellas at Polish people.

"We could qualify tonight already if things go our way," Dad said, as we walked towards the pub where we were meeting everybody. "I hope so, I don't want a nail-biter against Poland on Wednesday," I replied, slightly out of breath, as my dad was an insanely fast walker. It always felt like we had just robbed someone and were trying to get away as quick as possible without actually running.

We hadn't seen everyone since Denmark, and I had to admit that I was a bit nervous. We were on British turf now, and this is where they all lived and grew up. We didn't. We were some oddballs from another country who had decided that this was something we were going to be a part of. I had never wished I was English quite this much before. I felt like the anxiety about being questioned almost took over the joy of being here. It turns out I worried for nothing. The second we walked into the pub we were instantly greeted by familiar faces and pats on the back. Most of the people we met over in Denmark was here, but there were a lot of new faces too and what felt like a five minute conversation turned into hours. I finally got to meet Perry, who I knew from the forum but not in person. We were only teenagers back then, but what we didn't know was that we would come to form a bond throughout the years that would see future us going games together with my son as responsible adults. It's crazy how time flies when you're chatting football. When dad declared we had to start making our way to the ground I could of swore we had been there under an hour. We hadn't - it was close to five hours, and I think the amount of beer consumed may have been a contributing factor as to why I had lost all sense of time.

The walk to Old Trafford was magical. Now that's going to sound silly because it's just a walk, but for me it was more. I was a teenager living the dream I had since I was 12: going to England to watch football. Being part of the very same crowd I had watched chanting on the TV years ago. As we got into our seats and finally had a chance to soak up the atmosphere, I felt at home. Home to me had never been a place as such but more of a feeling. I felt that feeling where I stood that mild Saturday in October watching the team warm up.

As the anthem faded out and the game kicked off, I was a bag of
nerves. I had never seen England win before, and I was prematurely
imagining what it would feel like. We didn't start the game in the
most reassuring way, and we looked shaky the first 20. When we got
a penalty, I was praying Beckham wasn't taking it. He had missed
his last three penalties and it felt like we really needed this lead. The
irony of it all was that I refused to wear my glasses in public and so
when we stepped up to take the pen I couldn't for my life see who it
was.
We scored and Old Trafford absolutely erupted; we got thrown into
a pile, and as we emerged I turned to dad in confusion
"So who scored for us?"
Dad still claims that it made him laugh and afterwards he insisted on
me going to the optician.
Despite the goal we looked weirdly lethargic and there was no real
energy on the pitch.
Just a min into second half and it looked like Austria was levelling
but it hit the bar.
Shortly after Beckham got a second yellow card and was sent off,
much to our despair.
I think this game will forever be remembered as the time I used the
C word for the first time. Being foreign I had no idea what a frowned
upon word that was and so when I belted it out at the top of my
voice, I had several people turning around in absolute disgust at me.
Must be Austrian, I thought to myself, blissfully unaware of the way
I had misused the English language.
England managed to hold on to their 1-0 lead with 10 men, and when
the final whistle blew we all celebrated on top of each other, the fact
I had linguistically disgraced myself 30 minutes prior was already
forgotten.

"First home game we've been to and England wins - what a night!"
said Dad triumphantly as we walked out of the stadium and towards
the after party. I say walked but I mean ran, of course. 50% of my
calf strength comes from walks with my father.

"If Holland beat Czech Republic we've qualified," he continued, digging for something in his pocket. I was praying it wasn't another map.

The night was of epic proportions, as we found out Holland won their game and we had qualified we had all the more reason to celebrate. Denny spilt beer all over Dad's coat and we were pouring beer into each other's mouths laying on the floor. It was a night of many laughs and antics.
Me and Dad didn't say much on our walk back from the pub; it was the early hours and the streets had emptied out a bit. I was carrying my shoes in my hand for some reason and the concrete slabs felt cold underneath my feet. We were tired but victorious. There was no need for any conversation really. The night itself had spoken.
"I was going to say we will sleep well tonight, but given the beds I guess that's impossible," I joked, as we closed the door behind us.

The following days before the next qualifying game were spent getting lost in various areas of Manchester, Dad using a map, Dad insisting a dry baguette eaten while sat on the ground was luxury lunch, light delusional jogs, despair at the hotel, and of course a lot of anticipation ahead of the next game. I was really set on winning the group and so for me, the Poland game still had a lot of importance. We were drinking in the same pub ahead of this game and so was everyone else. There's comfort in the predictability of the match day in a way. You know beforehand how it's going to play out. The "Oh we better leave for the ground now" followed by the " we'll have time for one for the road first though" conversations, the drunk walk to the stadium where everything all of a sudden seems magic even though it's a rainy Wednesday in October. You know how it's going to be even before you've opened the door to the pub and someone asks you what you're drinking. This day had some slightly different elements to it but we didn't know that when we took that first sip of beer.

There's always a hostile atmosphere when we play Poland and today was no different. As we left the pub briefly to go and collect our

24

tickets with Perry, we noticed how Polish fans had started to gather outside the pub. Due to the fact Dad always ran rather than walked we weren't gone for too long, but it had proven to be long enough. We returned to a nasty atmosphere, and the Polish had bricked the pub. We tried to hurry in, but the stern bouncer was having none of it.

"No one comes in," he said, trying to hide the fact he was secretly loving the power. We tried to explain that everyone else was inside and that we had just popped out briefly, but he wasn't going to budge. We were not going to be let in. I didn't take the news very well and started shouting at the bouncer. Dad dragged me away, fully knowing that was a fight I was never going to win.
"I guess we'll have to go to the ground early instead," said Dad, and as it started raining heavily, he took his umbrella out. As we were approaching a tunnel, a group of Poland fans felt the need to start taunting us. You know a fan base are bad if they feel that it's necessary to start provoking a teen girl and her father. We were having none of it however. As they were getting closer, testing the boundaries of how close up our faces they could get, Dad took his brolly and wacked a Polish fan around the head. I say Dad but it might have been me. For the purpose of maintaining my good reputation, let's say it was Dad. For the purpose of my Dad's immaculate reputation, he claims it was me.
Guess we'll never know. We swiftly slipped into the massive crowds and continued to walk as if nothing had happened. Nothing deepens the father-daughter connection quite as much as a bit of low key umbrella violence on a rainy afternoon.

Inside the ground the atmosphere was continuously hostile, and I felt even more than before that a win was needed. Ending our week in England by winning our qualifying group felt like the end we deserved, especially after having the Polish taking liberties on our home soil. Some would argue me and Dad belonged as little here as the Polish, but that's a different conversation for another day.

The game didn't disappoint: we went 1-0 up with Owen, but Poland equalised.

We looked like a completely different team than over the weekend against Austria and we held possession and passing. As frustrating as it was, we just couldn't seem to score. I started to fret and contemplating maybe using the C- word for a second time this week - but things quickly changed.

When there was 10 mins left, we strung up a counterattack which Lampard clinically finished off and sent us into top spot of the group. Me and Dad celebrated in the cold October rain and life felt like it couldn't get better. What an end to the trip, and what an end to the qualifying campaign. World Cup 2006 awaited - and Dad didn't know it, but I already had elaborate plans for us. We celebrated all night, but as we stumbled into bed one last time in the godforsaken hotel, I couldn't drift off. Maybe it was the fact the room was along a busy main road or the fact my Dad was pulling timber like never before, but the main factor was my beating heart.

I had fallen in love with English football when I turned 12, and as naively as it sounded then, declared to everybody around me that I would be part of that life one day. Now I was, and it seemed almost surreal. We had, despite being foreigners, encountered minimal hostility. Instead, the British had welcomed us with open arms, made us into mascots, almost. We were the Swedes who followed England. I smiled to myself as I finally started to drift off. We were miles from Sweden, but in a much more real sense we were home.

Chapter 4

Germany 06; apple wine is quite alright

Almost a year after our debut at Rosie McGee's we were no longer newcomers. After our epic trip to Manchester I ventured on my first away game alone to Geneva. Dad declared that a friendly in Geneva a cold winter evening wasn't something he was subjecting himself to, guess he was still exhausted from swinging at the polish in Manchester, and so I went on my own. I met up with Perry, Denny and the rest over there. I had never travelled alone before and I remember having to run through Copenhagen airport to catch my connecting flight. Luckily I had plenty of practice from all my runs with my dear father and I made the flight with 5 minutes to spare. We were playing Argentina and the atmosphere had been absolutely rocking. Me and my mates had danced on tables and a few of them spent far too many nights in the epic gay club that was Manpower. Baxter had saved me from getting my head kicked in at the bar afterwards, someone had fallen down the stairs and I had fallen even further in love with the football. I was truly in it now. I cared about nothing else. I broke up with my long term boyfriend because he wasn't into football and it now consumed my whole life. The friends from the football was my family and we spoke almost every day online, me in Sweden and them over in England. An idea that perhaps I should move to England slowly started to form in my head but I was too scared to act on it. I had blown my education, and all my savings were currently being spent on football.

Me and my dad had spent 6 months planning the World Cup. England Fans ran a caps system for their tickets; you were given caps for each game you went to and the more caps the better chance of getting a ticket to the games that had a big interest. As we were still fairly new we didn't have enough caps to actually get tickets to the World Cup games but decided to go over anyway for the atmosphere.

"You're not right in your heads, are you?" Mum exclaimed one day whilst listening to me and dad planning to stay in Germany for a whole month. She was a football widow who was now losing her daughter as well. My brother was into football, but since me and my dad became over invested he just couldn't be bothered to even try to keep up with us. I was a passionate soul. I did everything 110% or not at all. There was no in-between. It was my best and worst trait.

The week before we headed off to Germany I went and got my first ever tattoo. This was back in 2006 before the whole tattoo trend had exploded and every man and their dog had a tattoo.

I remember a woman who people claimed was blind doing it on me in some sort of dark back alley setting. It wasn't classy but social status meant nothing to me. I was so wrapped up in the football. I left the tattoo studio that day with the words " Forever England" tattooed on my inner forearm. I was in it for life. This marriage would not end. Germany awaited.

"You fucking English scum!" The words echoed around the streets of Frankfurt as we got out of the train station. We had travelled all day and it was sweltering hot. We had a months' worth of luggage to drag around and the initial welcome package Germany was giving us was not wanted.

I casually flipped them the finger whilst trying to not drop all my luggage and they all just laughed. Guess little girl me wasn't really that intimidating. I've seen my dad swing golf clubs around in rage though, so I would stay clear of us if I was them.

We had rented a nice apartment in the city centre of Frankfurt and planned to watch the games in the large Fan Park down the river. Frankfurt was a beautiful city and once we had settled in and was heading down the pub life felt good again.

The first night in Frankfurt was crazy, we hadn't met any of the usual suspects yet but a bunch of lads from Birmingham became our friends for the night. They were all topless and smelt incredibly bad. They explained that they were all sleeping in their car.

We spent the night singing and dancing as normal and my dad got drunk on the local apple wine that he insisted on buying down the underground and smuggling up into the Irish bar. He would walk down the stairs into the toilets with his empty pint glass and refill it with his apple wine he carried around in his brief case. Yes dad had sort of a briefcase - but in a fabric version that was to become infamous on all our trips. It was not a football day out unless dad carried his bag with all his essentials in there. By essentials I mean apple wine in this case. Loads of it as well. I'm sure Germany's apple wine sale went up by 50% during our visit in Germany.

Most nights looked the same to be honest and I'm not going to bore you with a months' worth of the same stories from the inside of an Irish bar. Mainly because many of them are a little bit erm…shall we say blurry? I had a friend from the states called Fay and we met up with her for most of the games. England's first game was against Paraguay on the 10th of June.

In order to get a seat in the Fan Park you had to be there early, so even though England's kick off wasn't until 3 pm we found ourselves in the queue for when they opened at 10.

The fan park was laid out like a stadium. The big screen was in the water and they had raised stands all around it and there were beer stands dotted across the green areas. It was a really hot day and me and dad were sweating in the direct sun the second we took our seats. We consumed many beers that day in order not to die in the sun. It was a long day but the excitement to watch the game on the big screen along with all other ticketless England fans was taking over. I had never been to a tournament before and this was big to me. Despite not being at the actual game I was still part of it all. The atmosphere before and after was superb and my liver was already tired of me.
During the national anthem dad nudged me and held his arm out.

"Look, goosebumps again" I laughed, this man was extremely

patriotic when you came to think about it - just not for his homeland!

It only took 3 mins before Paraguay had managed to score an own goal and the stand at the fan park exploded. It was a sea of sweaty bodies on top of each other and I remember spilling beer all over the lad in front of me who just laughed and offered me his.

It probably wasn't our best game to be honest, but no one cared, we were winning. Towards the end of the second half the heat was bad and everyone had been in it for hours. This resulted in the fire services having to come by at the back and spray water all over us on the stand. We all started jumping up and down on the stand singing whilst the water soaked us to the core; my dad's watch got water damaged and stopped and my sun cream ran into my eyes so bad I couldn't see the big screen anymore. It was a glorious moment.

After winning the first game we spent all night celebrating with the other England fans. If I'm honest we got quite leery and it would be wrong for me to continue my account of that night as some of the details seems to have slipped my mind; probably all that sun, nothing to do with apple wine. Dad would agree.

The next game was 5 days later against Trinidad and Tobago. This was a 6pm kick off so we was spared from the worst of the sun. A heatwave seemed to have hit Germany during the World Cup and it was over 32 degrees most of the days. We had been there for a week now and even though my liver was crying my heart was happy. I had spent time with old faces and new faces and dad had way more than his recommended 5 a day through all that apple wine.

Trinidad and Tobago proved to be a bit of a hard nut to crack. After 80 mins it was still goal-less and I was losing my temper a bit in the stand.

"What are we even doing here if we can't beat Trinidad and fucking Tobago," I cursed to myself whilst downing some German budget beer my dad had smuggled into the stands. Was he out of apple wine finally?

Dad remained silent. He was very difficult when football went bad. He would just go dead quiet and not say a word and that silence was sometimes worse than the rage.

All of a sudden Crouch happened. In the 83 min he banged in our first goal and all of a sudden life was good again. All that criticism I had minutes earlier was washed away with the goal. It was always like that in football. The line between heaven and hell were thin and you often balanced on it for 90 minutes.

On overtime Gerrard shut the game down and we won 2-0.

No goals conceded yet and no losses, it was looking pretty good ahead of the last game of the group stage.

We went straight to the pub to continue the drinking and on our walk back in the early hours of the morning I dropped all my stuff and ran straight into a fountain. I don't quite know why but I had always wanted to celebrate a football victory in a fountain so there I was, middle of the night in an empty fountain, splashing about like a big stranded whale. My dad stood by and watched with a bemused look on his face. Probably questioning where he had gone wrong bringing me up.

All of a sudden the sound of police sirens broke the silence of the night and I was quickly out of the water and alongside dad, we started a casual jog back to the apartment.

Unlucky for us we got lost and ended up running around in circles, something that really frustrated dad who claims to have a great sense of directions. We ended up having to ask some guard in a little tower and he was very puzzled at my drenched 3am look. Turned out we were minutes from the apartment and had been all along without realising. Back at the apartment my dad mumbled something about needing a break from apple wine before falling asleep.

Another 5 days later on the 20th of June it was time for our third and last group game.
For us this wasn't just any game. We were playing Sweden.

Just saying it out loud came with a certain sense of dread for us. Not because we were stuck between the two. There was no contest whatsoever; we were England through and through and Sweden in football meant nothing to us. That was the reason we hated playing Sweden though, the comments and assumptions that we were somehow also rooting for Sweden. Having to explain it to everyone over and over was tiring but I suppose in a sense we did kind of owe people an explanation as to why we were the way we were.

Dad was up early as usual on match day. I could hear him in the kitchen making what I could only presume was cereal. His face lit up as I appeared in the doorway.

"Big game today, Bell."

"Yeah I wouldn't want to be back home now, I've already had several texts from my mates about the game," I answered whilst looking down on my phone.

"A draw will be enough to win the group but I want to beat them, I'll never hear the end of it at work otherwise," Dad continued whilst crunching his cereals. It sounded like titanic hitting that dreaded iceberg.

It was a 9pm kick off which meant most day would be spent in the bar before heading to the Fan Park. I had already text Fay to meet in the Irish bar before the game. Fay was Russian but lived in America and supported England. She if anyone understood our choice and it was nice having her around. She was 10 years older than me and a bit like a big sister; very pretty and not at all awkward like I was.

We spent the day having a laugh in the bar and I spent at least 2 hours explaining to everyone that I did not have any sympathies with Sweden. Dad was dancing to Grease without a care in the world. Once in our seats we were nervous, England were top of the group and Sweden second. Winning the group meant facing Ecuador in the knock out stages. Being runner up meant you would face Germany on their home turf so a win or a draw was really vital tonight. For us more so than others I would presume.

England's first half was a battle as usual but we took the lead 10 mins before half time with an absolute banging goal by Joe Cole. Life was good. Dad smirked at me but we knew better than to get our hopes up just yet. Sweden equalised at the beginning of second half and after that England didn't impress on the pitch too much. Rooney who had played his first game from start since his injury was subbed off for Gerrard and chucked his boots in anger. Gerrard went on to score 2-1 with 5 mins left and we completely exploded. I was just typing out some sarky comment back to my Swedish mate and as I was about to press send, Henrik Larson equalised for Sweden in the 90th minute. On paper it didn't matter at all. We had won the group and would face Ecuador in 5 days.

For me and dad it felt a bit like an anti-climax though. We had been so close to finally be able to put the " Who's better, England or Sweden" to bed; but tonight wasn't the night.

As we got back and into bed my phone flashed with a text message from my friend back in Sweden.

"Guess we will see you in the euros in two years, maybe you're ready to beat us then."

England played Ecuador on a Sunday afternoon. I will try and keep it short as I do realise that my account of this tournament might start to become slightly repetitive; but if you were there that glorious summer you would say otherwise. It had been a great experience so far. We had met people and made friends for life. Me and dad had managed to have zero arguments, even after the nights I failed to come back home to the apartment and ended up at some wild after party in the German suburbs. We would just sit on the balcony and have our breakfast whilst overlooking the streets of Frankfurt and watch as the world slowly came back to life. The sound of the city waking up would drown out the sound of dad slurping cereals which believe me was a bonus. It sounds like a cliché but we were genuinely living the dream.

The match day against Ecuador was no different to the other match days, pub followed by the Fan Park with Fay and her mother who had joined us. She was a quiet woman and now, 15 years later, I can't remember her name or what she looked like. I just know that she was a mild mannered woman who spoke softly and calmly. The absolute opposite to me and my dad who were loud and gobby at football. She had a calming presence in the otherwise passionate environment. She offered me bottles of water during the game when I was nervous. This was the knock out stages and we were painfully aware that our trip could come to an end this Sunday evening.

We won the game against Ecuador after a goal by Beckham start of second half and I remember dad shouting to me across the crowd as we celebrated: "7 more days, we'll get to stay 7 more days at least!"

We celebrated all night dancing on tables and singing songs about the Germans that I can't repeat in this book but you're probably familiar with; the handy work referring to someone's Luftwaffe and someone's RAF.

I became ill after that game and spent the next few days coughing my insides up in bed. Dad had to bring me McDonald's back to the room where I was bed ridden. It was clear now that we would play Portugal in the quarter finals Saturday 1st of July. If you follow football you know the history behind playing them, especially the disaster that was Euro 2004 where they knocked us out in the quarter finals on penalties, an absolutely heart-breaking moment for us. I remember having left my nan's funeral early with dad just to rush back home for that game. It still hurt when I thought about it. Whilst lying in bed munching stale McDonald fries I begged Saturday would not be a repetition of that.

Match day arrived and this time both me and dad were really nervous. We usually spent the mornings chatting and playing England songs on the stereo but the atmosphere were different this Saturday morning. It had been almost a month since we arrived in Germany and it could all come to an end this afternoon. It was a 5pm kick off and I can't remember if we went the pub beforehand or not. The whole day seemed like a bit of a blur. The dream of winning a World Cup whilst we were there was 3 games away and we could almost taste it. Probably not dad though, all he tasted was apple wine.

We met both Fay and her mum in the Fan park. Fay looked at me where I was stood leaning against the bar waiting for a beer.

"Jesus you look pale mate, it'll be fine well beat them today I can feel it. It's time."

I laughed nervously. I was a girl of few words when it came to football and nerves. I went into my own head and stayed there.

Dad was no better. He sat on the stand with a look I can't quite describe but it was probably fear and excitement mixed together. Fay was the opposite, always happy and positive.

The match started. England had not impressed so far in the tournament and Sven Goran had promised a big performance tonight.

It was another hot afternoon around 30 degrees and England stood up to Portugal well.

First half ended 0-0 and dad sighed loudly

"This is a real battle - nerve wracking."

I remember looking at the image of my face in my pocket mirror in the toilets. I looked like I had seen a ghost. Sometimes I wish I had just gotten into girly stuff instead to save me from all this horrible football related stress. Then again, there was nothing in the world better than when we were winning though, so I guess it evened out. I was going to need to invest in make-up that covered the black bags under my eyes though if I intended to carry on my life as a football supporter for sure.

Second half kicked off and it wasn't long until Rooney who had been frustrated all game got sent off. He appeared to stamp on a players groin. We all protested wildly in the stands. Swear words and empty beer bottles were flying through the warm summer evening. I hurled a bottle at someone I suspected was Portugal. Its worth mentioning that these were plastic beer bottles. Fay grabbed my arm as if to say calm down but I was too far gone now. The frustration was taking over and the feeling of here we go again was swallowing me up. As he left the pitch it felt like someone had let the air out of me. So this is how it ends? We lose after having someone sent off again like 98.

Dad swore to himself and Fay offered a bottle of water that was declined. It didn't end there though, it appeared as if the lions had got a second wind. Roared on by the fantastic support from the fans on the stand they put up a battle that'll always be remembered. It was one of the tensest halves of football I've watched. My heart was pounding as if it wanted to burst out of my chest.

It went onto extra time and England's will to continue despite being a man short was nothing but remarkable. I remember thinking that I loved them so much.

Towards the end of extra time my hands were shaking in my lap.

"Please, please no penalties, not again."

My prayers were unanswered and the game was blown off. It was time for penalties. My dad stood up at the stand with an angry look.

"I'm not fucking watching this. I know how it'll end." And just like that he was gone. I didn't even have time to question where because the shoot-out was about to start. I don't know why but I had tears in my eyes. I hated this feeling and I didn't want it to end like this. Not again.

Fay took my hand and we stood up in the stand, eyes glaring at the big screen as the lads lined up ready to take their penalties. It was so quiet in the fan park I was convinced my heart beat could be heard.

"Please," I whispered quietly.

It didn't end well. Instead the world cup dream ended there.

Hargreaves was the only one who scored, both Lampard, Gerrard and Carraghers penalties were saved by Ricardo. I still remember the image of Ronaldo scoring and ending it all. Fay and her mum asked if I was coming with them but I was not ready to do anything. I sunk into my seat again. Wrapped my flag over me like a tent and I think I sat like that for a good 30 mins before I stood up and started walking along the river. The same river we had walked along a week back singing and celebrating the Ecuador win. I don't know how long that walk took me but it felt like hours. I think I laid on the grass at one point before some kids came and taunted me.

As I made a turn to walk back to the apartment I saw my dad.

He came marching down the street like an SS general and I wasn't expecting that at all. He usually went straight to bed after a loss. We looked at each other for a brief moment not mentioning the obvious heartache even though it was there like a big thick wall between us.

"I'm so glad I found you, I've booked a night train and a ferry home. I can't stay a moment longer."

I agreed with him. This place was associated with happiness and the hope of a world cup win; now that was gone it would be nothing but bittersweet to stay.

We walked back and packed in silence. The apartment seemed different now. For over 3 weeks it had held our hopes and dreams and apple wine and now it seemed unfamiliar and cold. The sound of dad crushing cereal like a woodcutter seemed distant. I took one last look at the empty rooms before closing the door behind us. Hearing the heavy door shut behind us felt symbolic.

We started walking down the same cobbled streets we had walked down a month ago after just arriving. It was a warm night and various fans from various countries was out and about. Their world cup dream was still alive but ours was over. I felt bitter towards them almost.

We didn't say a word to each other the whole trip back. What was there to say?

I still had a horrible cough and kept the whole carriage awake all night on the train back.
When we changed trains somewhere in Germany dad went and got me a burger king. I remember saying thank you and that was the first time I had spoken since back in Frankfurt unless you count my persistent coughing fits.

On the last train back after various trains and ferries I picked up a newspaper on my seat.
The second I opened it the big black headline " England's dream is over" hit me and I felt tears welling up again. I looked out the window whilst letting the newspaper slip down onto the floor.
The naive idea that England would win the world cup and we would be there to celebrate all night didn't want to leave my mind quite yet.
It's always the " what ifs" that get you the most isn't it?

Dad, who must of seen me crying behind my sunglasses, finally broke the silence.

"It's been one hell of an adventure, though hasn't it?"

I smiled for the first time since yesterday.

"It sure has, dad. And Germany will be in shortage of apple wine for a long, long time."

Chapter 5
Macedonia – Wild dogs and wild nights

"Skopje? I don't think I've ever heard about anyone going there," my colleague laughed as I told everyone I would need a few days off work to travel to Macedonia for England's Euro 2008 qualifier. It was September and the bitter taste after our World cup departure had finally settled.

It was now replaced with an almost naive belief that I could attend every single qualifier game. My mum would sigh endlessly as I spent the evenings at the kitchen table planning strange trips. My dad couldn't keep up either and settled for being dragged to the home games for now. My wallet was another component that wasn't quite keeping up but that's a whole other story.

I flew out to Macedonia alone from Sweden via Slovenia. When we transferred in Slovenia there was something wrong with the plane at take-off. I was already a nervous flyer and this didn't help. We were sat on the landing strip for ages before they announced that no fault could be detected and were ready to fly. It didn't feel very assuring and my hands were cramping from squeezing my handbag so tight. For someone who detested flying I sure subjected myself to a lot of it.

We made it there in one piece and I took a taxi from the airport to the hotel. I was sharing a room with my friends I've known since Geneva 05, DL, Max and Ted. We met up outside the hotel to check in and it was sweltering hot. Max was wearing some dumb "what goes on tour stays on tour" t-shirt and I told him nothing that goes on tour ever stays there and we all know that. We all went down the strip together and met up with all the other people we knew by now. I was relatively new still and Max who was far from a newbie kindly made sure I was introduced to every man and his dog.

It was a good night, the decade long joke about how DL (Daddy

Lover) only hits on fathers instead of daughters were born and I don't think we've ever seen him since without referencing it. We had spent the afternoon with some stunning local women but DL had shown no interest in them, instead he had proceeded to go on and on about their fathers, showing an almost unhealthy amount of personal interests in them. You can't do anything like that at football, you'll acquire a nickname forever. And as far as nicknames goes, Daddy Lover is probably not one you'd want.

It was only towards the end of the night that I for the first time encountered someone I didn't like. He started making comments about me not belonging there and being a fraud and it was really not what I needed to hear given the fact I had spent the last year emptying my bank account to be able to watch England. I knew him from the forum and he was one of those sly, sarcastic little shits who lives solemnly to wind others up. I probably shouldn't of raised to it but I was only 19, and having some middle aged man questioning my loyalties to the football made me tick over a bit and I said some things before walking off. That's all well and fine if you're somewhere familiar, but I certainly wasn't. I ended up lost in a Macedonian ghetto and this was before smart phones so I had no maps at hand. It was dark and seedy and a homeless man sleeping on a cardboard box kept shouting at me. He probably thought I was trying to invade his territory. I think he chased me at one point I wasn't brave enough to turn around and confirm but I could hear footsteps in the dark corners so I walked as fast as I could without blatantly running. Only problem was that I didn't know where I was going and it was dark so everything looked the same. I was quietly cursing myself for letting someone whose opinion I didn't even value get to me. It was just such a touchy subject to me. I felt that I had spent all my time and money following England and the fact some people still questioned why just didn't sit well with me. I was only a teenager, keen to fit into a picture I had always adored.

Max finally located me after a few phone calls and we decided that that's enough adventures for tonight.

"He's just a mouthy twat - who's he to question why I'm here?" I muttered as we walked back home.

Max just laughed. He had been around long enough to take no notice of people winding you up. I clearly had a lot to learn or I would be destined to get lost in foreign ghettos for the rest of my life.

"He wants to know if your father is anywhere nearby?" I told the Macedonian girl chatting to DL as we sat in the sunshine drinking beer before the game. She seemed puzzled and DL swore at me discretely. It was a new day and my irritation from last night was completely gone. More familiar faces from past trips had showed up and we had took over the strip once again. Perry was there and so was my friend Megan and her boyfriend. We were downing green shots and laughing all afternoon. Max tried push my buttons by asking where my beloved friend from last night were but I was not rising to it this time. You learn quick on these trips I guess. I had also learnt the ample art of downing pints as well I may add. Some Macedonian fans came and joined us and there was never any hostility. They wanted us to come to some big club after the game where their relative was having a birthday party. Max wasn't keen, but me and DL shrugged our shoulders and thought why not. DL was salivating at the idea of an evening in the company of fathers.

"He's wearing a bum bag, I'm not going to any party with him," Max laughed as we made our way to the stadium. A whole day of elegantly downing pints to keep up with the lads had gotten to my head but not in a bad way; quite the opposite. We were merrily shouting and chanting on our walk and I was loving being abroad with England. I had been to Geneva last year but this felt more like a proper trip, far away from home in some strange country watching football and having a laugh. I didn't need much more from life; I really didn't.

Inside the stadium we were all packed together in a corner and the atmosphere was brilliant.
When crouch scored in the first minute of second half things felt even better. The large man next to me picked me up and my legs accidentally kicked the man in-front of me. I apologised profusely but he just laughed.

"It's not a football game unless someone kicks ya, is it?" he laughed and winked at me.

England ended up winning 0-1 and we were happy with that. McLaren had took over after Sven-Goran left after the World cup and he wasn't exactly someone we had any faith in.

We made our way back to the strip after the game to find the Macedonian lads with the dreaded bum bags. They were waiting for us in the bar and we had a few drinks before Max and Ted went off somewhere else. Me and DL tagged along to this rather spectacular open ceiling night club in the middle of absolutely nowhere. It looked like dessert surrounded us but we had little concerns about that. The drinks were flowing and England had won. DL was surrounded by fathers and life was good. We posed for several pictures together with a Macedonian family and the idea that their photo album from their uncles birthday party would have two drunken football fans in it forever amused me.

It must have been around 4am when we left and started walking back. The sun was not yet up but the sky had changed from night dark to morning light. Christian, the Macedonian lad with a bum-bag, was guiding us back to our hotel seeing as we had no clue where we were. He took us through a park and all of a sudden a large pack of wild dogs appeared ahead of us. I guess we were on their territory. There was quite a few of them and we all slowed down. I was unsure what was to happen next and judging by DL so was he. My heart was pounding, I was tired from a whole day of drinking and not at all in a fit state to fight wild dogs. We both looked at Christian for some sort of guidance. He smiled and opened the zip on his beloved bum-bag and took out a canister of what looked like pepper spray or similar. Great, just great. We were in the middle of nowhere about to start pepper spraying ferocious wild dogs. He held the can out and casually let a few sprays out to warn the dogs. I held my breathe. The dogs didn't seem at all intimidated but kept coming closer and closer to us. Christian who seemed like this was something he did everyday just laughed and went "Run", and we did. We absolutely legged it down the side bit of the park. Christian was still leading the way with me and DL close behind him as we ran through the night.

Did the dogs chase us? Not a clue. You'd be really dumb to stop and turn around at that point wouldn't you?

We could hear distant barking however and that was enough to keep running. When we finally reached what appeared to be civilisation I had to stop and lean on DL to catch my breathe. It was safe to say we had not took a brisk morning jog into consideration when we spent all night caning beers and stuffing our faces with the uncle's buffet food. Christian who apparently was in the form of his life appeared unaffected. He put his little spray back in his bum-bag and hugged us goodbye. I hope he didn't feel how drenched my back was from sweat. Me and DL continued the short walk to the hotel.

"At least we know why he wears that bum-bag now eh, to save football fans from wild dogs," DL laughed as we walked through the lobby. I laughed with him, another game ticked off the list and another story to add to the memory box. I was wondering what my friends did back home right now? Probably not getting prepared to fight wild dogs after a Macedonian middle aged man's birthday bash, that's for sure. We slept well that night. DL dreaming about fathers and me wild dogs.

"We're sorry but the flight are delayed, please see check in desk for more information."

I sighed. I was sat in a cramped airport lounge in Slovenia waiting for my connection flight back to Copenhagen. I had an evening coach to catch from Copenhagen to Sweden, and I really couldn't afford a delay as it was the last coach going back. I had work in the morning and needed to sleep this trip off for sure. One of the lads I knew from the forum, Todd, who I always said hello to was on the same flight. He waved me over and told me he had access to the executive lounge so we went in there amongst all the businessmen. Two tired and worn out football fans inside the corporate world. I had spent the afternoon in the pub with the rest and I was running on very little sleep. The hangover from last night had me in a firm grip and I really didn't want to get stuck in Ljubljana. Todd proceeded to tell me about how he had his car parked at Copenhagen airport and he was driving to Sweden for a work thing. He told me he could give me a lift to one of the cities down south and I could sleep at the train station and take the first train back in the morning. It didn't sound ideal but it was better than being stuck in Copenhagen and at least I be back on Swedish soil and a little bit closer to my final destination. My phone battery was about to die and I had no Swedish money on me, but I was sure I'd figure out a way to get from one city to another once I was back in Sweden. I text mum and told her we were delayed and I would miss my coach from Copenhagen and informed her of my revised plan.

"Are you mad? I don't like the sound of this at all - do you even know this guy who's car you're getting into?" Poor mum, every single wrinkle she gained during the last decade was down to me, I was sure of it. I had always had a strange way of getting myself out of the situations I got myself into though. It was never straight forward but I always ended up fine. I was sure this was no exception. Todd was a very calm gentle man and didn't look like he had elaborate plans to murder me at all. He was too tired from Macedonia and murdering seems like an effort. I was most certainly safe.

After hours and hours of delay we finally touched down in Copenhagen. I struggled to stay awake in the car over the bridge from Denmark to Sweden. Todd was a man of facts and he had a fact about every single thing in the world. It was like cruising through the night with David Attenborough. We got to the train station around 2am in the morning. It wasn't officially open but it was still unlocked. Seemed like a bad idea to leave an empty train station unlocked; but it was so small it could barely be called a station anyway. I said bye and thanks to Todd and made my way inside. It was dark and a bit creepy in there. The sound of the escalators going up and down didn't help the horror film factor. I was expecting a creature to appear up the escalator at any time. I sat down on the bench the furthest away from the doors and escalators and started looking through my camera and all the pictures I had took. I liked doing that

44

on my way back from a trip. It sort of put life back into the memories. I laughed loudly to myself as pictures of DL posing with a bunch of Macedonian fathers flashed by. There was a lot of noise outside at one point and I really didn't want any trouble so I gave up and took my bag into the toilets. They were coin toilets but I had some shrapnel at the bottom of my bag that wasn't Macedonian. I went into the disabled one and set up camp for the night. Somehow the fact I was curled up on a dirty bathroom floor with my backpack as a pillow didn't seem that strange anymore. I must of eventually drifted off to sleep because I woke up abruptly by a lot of rattling and voices outside the toilet door. I looked at my watch. It was 5 in the morning and it sounded like the cleaners were here to clean the station before it opened. I stood up and splashed some water on my face. It didn't help at all. I looked awful and the stress over having no money or a ticket to get back was starting to create a bit of quiet despair within my hungover self. I opened the door and the cleaner looked at me as if she had just seen a ghost. I nodded at her and smiled before quickly leaving the toilets. I didn't want any questions or conversation.

When the station finally opened at 6am I went into one of the little kiosks to ask if I could borrow their phone. He seemed unnecessarily suspicious and it annoyed me. I was so tired and I really didn't need a third degree as to why I needed to borrow the phone. I quickly called my dad's work number, as he would be at work by now. The man insisted on breathing down my neck as I waited for dad to pick up. His breathe smelt of coffee and cigarettes.

"Belle, what sort of ordeal have you got yourself into now eh?" Dad laughed the second he heard my voice. I explained I had no money and no phone and I was stuck. My dad was prepared for the call and proceeded to tell me he had put money onto my card and there was a train leaving in 30 mins platform 5. Bless my dad; efficiency was his forte.

"But the ticket office isn't open yet dad - I can't buy a ticket for the train," I said and gave the shop owner a look as he was now literally sat in my lap. Guess I could charge him for a lap dance and use that for train fare.

"Just get on the train and explain to them what's happened and buy the ticket on the train."

We hung up and I left the kiosk after giving the owner a dirty look.

I went down to the platform and the train was already in. I got on it and waited for someone that looked like a conductor to appear. A man eventually came down the aisle and I cleared my throat and asked him to buy a ticket. I guess the fact I looked like I was homeless didn't help my case.

"You cannot do that here miss, you have to buy them before boarding the train."

I started to explain my situation with despair in my voice but he was having none of it. I had to go wait for the ticket office to open. I delivered my second dirty look of the day as I walked off the train. This must have been the longest it's ever took someone to get back from anywhere ever.

The ticket hatch eventually opened and I was able to ask them about the next train to my city and buy a ticket for it. The relief when I finally sat down on the right train with a valid ticket was immense. I was meant to be back at work today but that wasn't going to happen. I very much doubted my boss would want me coming in straight from a 3 day bender in Macedonia.

I smiled to myself when the train left the station and I allowed my mind to re-visit the trip. Despite the obvious hiccups it had really been one hell of a trip. I had laughed non-stop and the memories would last me a life time. If someone had told me all those years back that the football would take me on all these crazy trips around the world I would of started it sooner. I couldn't think of a reason good enough to not wanting to do this always. I wanted to have kids eventually and take them to games. Maybe I could avoid wild dogs and sleeping in toilets at that stage though. As I walked through the door a day later than planned my mum appeared in the hall. Her face was a mix of bemusement and disbelief as she watched my tired face crash onto my bed, still wearing last night's clothes with various stains down the top.

"Surely you've had enough of this now for a while?"

I turned around from where I was lying in bed face down into my pillow and gave mum a coy smile.

"What you're witnessing right now is only the beginning, mother. It's only the beginning."

Chapter 6
Euro 08 campaign, McLaren out

"I don't think you should go to Russia. You've been everywhere the past year, I'm constantly worried."

My mum looked at me across the table as I was filling in my Russian Visa application for a 3 day stay in Moscow for England's qualifier against Russia 07. She was right. I had been everywhere the past year. I think mum expected me to be put off after Macedonia and the string of missed flights, trains, sleeping rough and missing days of work. I wasn't, instead it had spurred me on to want to go to even more trips. I had the football fever and I had it bad. No paracetamol in the world could cure it.

A month after Macedonia away I dragged Dad with me to Manchester to watch England's home game against Macedonia. It was an absolute farce of a 0-0 draw and I lost Dad in Manchester. We never booked a hotel and intended to sleep at the airport and catch the morning flight back.
I went the pub where all our mates were and he wasn't there. I remember thinking where would a Swedish man with no phone be in Manchester? In the end I gave up and went to the airport. It was just gone midnight and as I walked into the departure lounge the first face I spot was my dad's.

He was casually sat on a bench as if he had not been missing for 10 hours straight.

We laughed at each other. What an incredibly unnecessary trip this had been. When we curled up on the hard airport chairs to sleep dad was complaining about the security announcements keeping us awake. I laughed and said something he claims to always think about when he's in the middle of one of my dumb adventures.

"Come on dad, most people at your age spend their Saturdays at home playing bingo, you're sleeping on an airport chair after being lost in Manchester all day - how many men of your age have adventures like that?"

He laughed and we drifted off to the monotone voice of the woman over the speaker system telling us to keep our luggage with us at all times. Would have been handier if they reminded us to keep our fathers with us at all times.

I ended 2006's football trips with a friendly in Holland. It was November and absolutely freezing and I didn't bring a warm jacket. I never booked a hotel, I just flew over, went to the game, went to the pub and then straight to the airport and onto my 6am flight back. It was the shortest trip I had done so far but nonetheless a nice end to a superb football year. I raised my glass on new years eve to a whole new year of football.

2007 arrived and I started it with a pointless trip over to Manchester in February for a friendly against Spain who won 0-1. I met my future best mate Chess on this trip - but you'll hear more about him later on. I also sat next to Swedish football star Henrik Larson on the flight to Manchester. I told him his recent goal had been a clear offside. Strangely enough, we had a really good time on the plane. More than anything, he was baffled that I supported England whilst being Swedish. I'm sure he went back to training camp that afternoon telling them all about this strange girl he sat next to on the flight.

I then went to Barcelona in March for England's qualifier against Andorra. We won 3-0 but the first half was so woefully bad we booed the team off the pitch for the first time I can remember. I don't usually boo the love of my life but at this point we all had enough of McLaren's hapless tactics and his dumb umbrella. We shut the bars down after the game and as me, Perry and DL all shared a room; the reception called me down and implied that I was holding some sort of orgy. It didn't help that Denny was randomly also in our room at one point, and I have to admit it looked a bit dodgy, but I can assure you there was nothing like that going on. The reality was far less exciting and it was essentially just all of us drunkenly crashing into bed. DL slept at the bottom of the bed like a loyal dog. Presumably there was little on offer in the father department in Barcelona.

In the summer the same year I went over to London as Wembley was reopening again. We played a first game against Brazil there and it was a 1-1 draw. My mate Zeb paid 9 quid for a burger at Wembley; we drank a lot and people kept mistaking Chess's brother for Richard Keys. I stayed at Chess's the days before the game and as the airport lost my luggage I had to wear his clothes for the duration. We went to Windsor castle in matching outfits.

I think I had time to fly back to Sweden and change clothes before me and dad were heading over to Estonia for yet another away game. My dad's first this campaign. We went on a cruise from Sweden to Tallinn.

"I can't believe you're missing your son's and brother's graduation," Mum muttered at us as we waved goodbye. The trip to Tallinn was another one to remember. It was 32 degrees, the square was filled with drinking England fans and someone called Buster took me to a backstreet off license and I'm pretty sure we robbed the place. I remember him asking me to wait outside whilst he went inside; when he returned he chucked me a massive bag with beers and we half jogged down the streets of Tallinn. We would have ran faster but Buster was a large lad and I had left my shoes at the square.

I remember looking at his neck jiggling as he ran - he must have had at least 5 neck rolls and as he was topless it was all out on display, the sweat on his ample chest was glistening in the sun. It shouldn't have but it made me thirsty.

When we got back we handed out cans to everyone on the square and despite the restaurants and bars telling us we couldn't drink our own stuff in there we did. The Estonian people walked past the square shaking their heads. The very attractive Estonian women were constantly harassed and I'm
sure I was shouting things as well; it's easy to get drawn into the atmosphere. That's my excuse anyway. This was one of the few games me and dad had not managed to get tickets for. Instead I had

gone out of my way to get some off the record. I got banned on the Estonian forum after applying for a job as a mascot and then pretending I was a journalist and asking for access to the stadium during the game. In the end I got hold of an Estonian lad on another forum and we decided to meet up in Tallinn and exchange money for tickets. We were very nervous in case he wasn't showing up or in case the tickets were fake.

"Can't believe we are doing this," Dad said to me as we stood at a street corner in Estonia. A car with dark windows slowly pulled up and waved us over. We paid way more than the tickets were worth but desperation comes at a price. When we put the tickets through the detector waiting for them to flash green my heart was beating like crazy, but they turned out to be legit.

England had one of their better games and won 3-0. They had not impressed at all this campaign and we wasn't sure if we would even qualify, so this felt good.

The rest of our Estonian trip involved a horrible hangover, a strip club, stealing a wheelchair at 4am in the morning and watching my dad yet again dance to *Grease Lightning*.

On the ferry home I was in a bad way. My dad wasn't. I didn't get what calibre he was made of but I wanted to grow up and be like him. He left me in a foetal position in the hut and went down the dance floor and drank. When he got back in I was half asleep trying to ignore sea sickness mixed with a 4 day hangover. He whistled some dumb limbo tune from their entertainment and I huffed at him.

" Don't worry Bell; one day you'll be able to keep up with the best."

I had also started following a club team the past year, and it was Luton Town who I had always had a soft spot for. I flew over for a few games and after Estonia I went on a 30 hour coach trip alone to Norway for Luton's pre-season tour. The games got called off due to a flooded pitch and I was stuck in Stavanger for a week. I knew some lads from Luton and we made the most of the week by drinking in the pub. When it was time to go home I showed up to the coach station and realised that dad had booked the wrong day back, so I had to return to my hotel and book another night. All in all I spent another 35 hours to get home and my mum was shaking her head in utter disbelief. As if England games wasn't enough I had now added a club team to my repertoire. I only existed through football. Anything else was of irrelevance to me.

In September me and dad went to London for a week for the games against Israel and Russia. We met up with Fay and her mum for the first time since Germany; we talked memories, I introduced her to all my football mates, and we mocked her a bit for buying a half and half scarf. England won both their games 3-0 and it was finally starting to look up for us. The only thing that wasn't looking up for us was the absolute shit tip of a hotel my dad had booked us for the week. Try and imagine Faulty towers but even more comical. I felt like I was infected with something for sure by the time we left.

When we got back my mum presumed that this was enough; but it wasn't. I had two more trips planned this year. Fly over to London on a Saturday for England's home game against Estonia, back home and work for a day before I was headed off to Moscow on the Tuesday.

I had acted a bit hasty and managed to book a hotel in Moscow far away from everyone else meaning that I would actually be alone in Russia, a place we had been told by the FA not to be alone in. I didn't think anything of it. Most of the time it was just propaganda. The media loved to make out that every England away game was a battlefield and that we were always fighting.

I had seen nothing the past 2 years and I was convincing my mum that it would be absolutely safe.
I would fly over to Moscow, get a taxi from the airport to the hotel and then go meet up with my friends in the pub as usual.

What could possibly go wrong?

Chapter 7
Moscow; it only hurts when I cough
Part 1

I looked around the airport slightly puzzled. I had slept on the flight and was still waking up. All gates and directions on the board were in Russian. I swore to myself for not taking that as a second language back in school. My rusty German was useless right now. The queue to the visa check was endless and full of impatient football fans wanting to go to the pub. The guards with weapons felt a bit excessive. I had never heard about a massacre in a visa queue.

After what I could only presume was half a day I was finally out on the other side. There was a steady stream of football fans walking towards the exit and I just followed.

We had strict instructions from the fan embassy what taxis were safe to use. Yellow ones called Moscab were the only safe ones. I had walked out of airports in many strange countries and just took a taxi without as much as a worry so I guess my alert wasn't as high as it should have been. My focus was solemnly on that first sip of beer in the pub whilst listening to one of my mates antics from last night, most likely young Zeb's.

The second I stepped outside, a man in a black leather jacket with grey hair and a lanyard with a photo came up to me. He showed his ID badge quickly and said "Taxi?" in broken English. I looked around for the yellow cabs and there were loads of them so I presumed we were going into one of them. I nodded and followed him. When he stopped at a non-yellow car without any taxi sign on it, I hesitated, but for some reason found myself getting into it. Thinking back at it, I don't know what I was thinking, but I guess I was naturally non suspicious of things and didn't want to feel like a silly paranoid little girl. The second we started driving I regretted getting into the car. I tried to show him a piece of paper with my hotel address on but he just did thumbs up without looking. I

remember saying " Do you know where this hotel is?" but he turned
the strange Russian techno music up rather than answering. I was a
little bit worried now.

You know when you get that feeling that something isn't quite right
but you don't know if it's your wild imagination playing games with
you? Surely I wasn't in danger for real? Those things only happen on
the silver screen. I remember a film called *Lilja 4-ever* that we
watched in school about Russian sex slavery, and how many girls
were abducted in cars and forced to sell themselves. I shook my head;
that wasn't what was happening right now. I was at an England away
game not some strange abduction journey. I tried to relax and enjoy
the view of the snowy Russian landscape outside the car window.

I had looked up the journey time from the airport to my hotel
beforehand and it wasn't that far. When I looked at my phone screen
I realised that we had been driving for 40 minutes now and appeared
to be out of civilisation. It was at this point my real panic started to
set in. It was still mixed with absolute disbelief however. I text my
friend Fay from Russia to ask what she thought about it all. Was I
being paranoid?

A reply flashed on my screen and my shaky hands fumbled to get the
text up. I won't forget what it said.

"Get out of the car now. I'm being serious."

My heart started pounding. Get out of the car? How? Up until this
moment I had took comfort in the fact I was being paranoid but that
was all gone now. This appeared to be very real. I text my best mate
Chess who I went the football with and was meeting up with later.
He said the same. Get out.
I text my mum and told her what was happening and to contact the
embassy if she never heard back from me. It felt like a bad dream
but I couldn't wake up.

I looked at the driver. He looked back at me in the rear view mirror
and I think today, over a decade later, I'd still be able to recognise
his eyes out of a hundred. He had a long weathered face and his eyes

were strangely sad. A plan started to form in my head. I was going to open the door and jump out as soon as he stopped at the next traffic light. There was only one problem. I couldn't figure out if he had locked the back doors or not. The little plug looked like it was unlocked but I'm not a car person and maybe Russian cars were different. If he was going to abduct me he would have locked the doors surely? Or would he leave them unlocked so that I wouldn't become suspicious? What if I tried to open the door and they were locked? He would probably get really mad. Making him mad didn't feel like something I wanted to do. That feeling of panic that I felt there and then is something that I have never ever felt again at that strength and intensity.

It was now clear that we were heading far out of town. I was becoming more and more sure of what needed to be done. I had been in this car 50 mins now and all the facts was pointing towards this not ending very well. The absurdness of the situation had me in a firm grip.

I looked out the window just in time to see a yellow Moscab swish by. It had a bunch of cheery England fans in it and I remember thinking how lucky they were to be in that car. Was I really about to get out of a car in the middle of nowhere in Russia? Was this really happening? I guess it was.

My heart was beating so loud I couldn't hear my thoughts as we slowed down approaching a big traffic light at some sort of cross road. There was a ditch on my side of the car and I decided that now might be my only chance. If he swapped lanes I would have no chance jumping out as I would get hit by cars from the other lanes. I could only do this if he was in the outside lane which he was.

I slowly slipped my phone into my pocket so I wouldn't lose it. He wasn't looking at me. He was fidgeting with something in the glove compartment waiting for the lights to turn green. He had a bunch of scrunched up rags in there. Probably to wash his car but my mind couldn't take this guessing game anymore.

The lights were still on red and I put one hand on the door handle and the other was hugging the bag. I was going to open the door and try pull the bag with me. I counted down from 3 in my head.

3..2..1..

It all happened so fast.

One second I was in the car, the next I was half stumbling down the side of the road and the force which I had pulled my bag with made the bag slam into me. I heard car horns sound but I didn't dare to look back. I got up and just walked. Walked, walked, walked. I presume he must have had to continue driving with his car door open and the idea of him pulling up somewhere to close it whilst I was still within reach made me sweat even though the temperature were below freezing.

What now? I was out of what was presumed to have been a nightmare car and was now walking along a long Russian road in the middle of nowhere. Little snowflakes were falling from the grey skies. Everything felt so surreal. The sort of stuff you read about happening to others and think to yourself: " You must be pretty naive to get into a situation like that."

So yeah, that was me right now. Naive, cold and lost in Moscow. It sounded like the name of a film I rather not watch to be honest.

I don't think it would have ended well if it wasn't for my mate Chess. I could write a novel about that lad and it still wouldn't be able to fit all the gratitude I had for him. Chess was selfless and always put others ahead of himself. I had gotten to know him at the beginning of the year during a friendly in Manchester; we had clicked instantly and he had been over to Sweden to visit us all back in August. I trusted him with my life. I text him the name of a metro station I had reached and he dropped everything and told me to stay where I was, he would come and find me. I went into a little packed McDonalds just next to the station and sat down to wait for him. I watched Russian teenagers laugh and joke around and I thought to myself that the contrasts can be so big. That could have been me now, laughing in the pub with my mates but instead I was lost in a Russian ghetto after getting out of a car in the middle of traffic. It probably took Chess over an hour to find me but the relief I felt when I saw his familiar face appear was overwhelming.

He couldn't believe what had happened and gave me a slight bollocking for getting into the absolute seediest car I could find. I really couldn't explain why I went into the car despite all alarm bells ringing but it was like I was conditioned to always ignore my gut feeling and write it off as paranoia. If this was meant to be some sort of lesson to trust my instincts I think it was a bit on the brutal side.

After a long catch up we shared a real taxi back to my hotel and he dropped me off. I told him I was going to skip the pub tonight. It was out of character for me to miss the pub the night before a game but I was completely drained. He understood, he always did. He had a sort of worried look on his face despite my reassurance that I was fine.

"Promise you'll be OK now? I'll stay if you want?"

I laughed at his overly concerned face and offer to sacrifice the magic that was the night before a game.

"Mate, I will be fine I promise. I'm just going to relax in my room - what could possibly go wrong?"

We said goodbye and I watched his taxi disappear into the cold Russian evening. I went into the hotel lobby with every intention of just sleeping the evening away.

Little did I know that Russia wasn't quite done with me yet.

Chapter 7
Moscow; it only hurts when I cough
Part 2

After I unpacked and showered the car journey off me I sat down on the questionable bed. The theme in the room appeared to be old communist Soviet. It was red and yellow and the bedspread looked like the kind of spread you use to hide a body in the woods. It had fag burns all over it and I decided to put it away. My tiny TV in the corner was showing some Russian game show and I was bored already. I looked at my phone. Various texts from my mum making sure I was OK. Usually I would be annoyed at her but this time her concern was more than justified after the afternoon we just had. I had some texts from my friends asking what the plan was tomorrow and I decided to give them a call. If anything it would kill time until I could sleep. I dialled my mates number but the bad reception kept cutting me off.

I walked down the hotel lobby to get phone reception but a leery group of fans were chanting so I walked outside instead. I wasn't wearing any colours; we had been told not to. I was however speaking English loudly on the phone and I guess that in itself was enough to make me a target.
Yet again, without knowing it, I had put myself in harm's way.

I don't know what happened next. The last thing I can remember is hearing loud voices shouting and a sharp pain in my head before it went sort of black. Not completely black because I could still hear voices and feel pain but it seemed distant. Like when you're sleeping on an airplane and are half asleep dreaming but also hear the surroundings. It felt like that. I wanted to open my eyes but couldn't. Next thing I knew I was inside. I had lost concept of time completely. Could be minutes, could be hours later.

I was laying on what appeared to be a bench. The lights were bright and a woman with a very stern face was dabbing my cheek with

what I can only presume was vodka. The strong smell felt like a
thick layer in my nose. Was I dead?

"What's happening?" My own voice sounded croaky and not at all
like me. I cleared my throat.
She didn't answer me. Her face was so close to me I could see all her
deep wrinkles. She looked like she had lived a hard life. He breathe
was a mix of cigarettes and mint. I didn't mind it.

She put a plaster on my cheek and I felt relieved. If whatever had
happened to my face could be fixed by a plaster it couldn't be that
bad.

"You're good," she said and nodded at me to stand up. I was thinking
to myself that I probably was far from good. If this was good I dread
to think what bad would feel like. My head was pounding as if
someone was repeatedly slamming a hammer into it and my ribs
were so sore it hurt to take a deep breath. I appeared to be in a little
side room behind the reception desk at the hotel and as I stumbled up
to leave she handed me a bag. It had my red little mobile phone in it
and my room key. I didn't like that; it looked like one of those crime
scene bags.

Confused and dazed I made my way out into the lobby. It was fairly
quiet now so I presumed it was that glorious time of the evening
when everyone were getting together in the pub. I could almost hear
the distant laughter and clinking of beer glasses.

A woman started walking towards me. She had a worried look on
her face and what I presumed was her husband sat on the sofa behind
her flicking through a brochure. She reminded me of a Swedish TV
presenter we all liked.

"Oh god I'm so glad to see you on your feet," she exclaimed. I was
still a bit confused. I understood that someone had attacked me
outside but I had no idea what the circumstances was. There was no
sign of any police or ambulance or any of the usual commotion that
follows an assault.

I sat down next to her and her husband on the sofa and she started telling me about what had happened. I listened and it felt like she was talking about someone else. I had a large lump in my throat but I couldn't cry. It felt like I left my body for a while.

She told me how her and her husband and two friends had gone outside to wait for their taxi. It pulled up at the bottom of the complex so they started walking towards it. When they turned round the corner they had seen some lads in Spartak Moscow scarves kicking what they thought was a dog on the ground.

Her husband and his friends ran towards them and they ran off before they got there. They called her over and she helped getting me inside. The hotel immediately took me to the back room and told the rest to stay back. She asked them to call the police and they nodded but never called evidently. When she asked another woman at the desk about me she pretended she knew nothing. I felt a chill down my spine. What was this backwards country?

"That's pretty much what we can tell you. There weren't that many people left in the lobby when it happened as most had left for the pub. I'm just so glad we were."

I swallowed. "Me too. I owe you a drink, I really fucking do."

She smiled and told me her name was Sonia. I never thought to exchange details as most of the times you just find people in pubs around the city. I was sure I would find her and her friends and buy them a drink tomorrow. Her husband who hadn't said a word up until now took a deep breath.

"Suppose we'd better be off, hopefully we'll see you tomorrow. No more trouble now eh?"

He smiled but it was one of those tired smiles. I guess his evening hadn't exactly been how he wanted it to be.

"Are you sure you're OK to go the game tomorrow? You've literally just taken a beating. Maybe try the hospital?" Sonia said as they were getting up to leave.

The idea of a Russian hospital sent shivers down my spine.

"I'll be fine - I don't think they got me that bad."

We said bye and her and her husband went outside yet again to wait for a taxi, this time less eventfully.

I went into the elevator and that was the first time I saw my face in the mirror. I had a cut on my nose and a big plaster on my cheek. My eyes looked puffy as if I had been crying but I hadn't.
Or had I? It all felt so fucking surreal. Something had happened to me that I couldn't even remember most of. All I had was a strangers story and little fragments of what I could remember. Maybe that was for the best.

When I got into my room I spotted what looked like the beginning of a large bruise on my rib cage. I guess that's where they had kicked me. I didn't fully process what had happened that day and evening at all. I felt like I had myself to blame for this. Getting into a car despite all the warnings. Walking around in the dark alone speaking English and making myself a super easy target.
I felt dumb. Why had they attacked me in such a cowardly way?
Had I been nothing but a warning to the rest? Was this the Russians way of letting everyone know that they had no issues attacking women, children or men?

My thoughts kept me awake for most of the night along with the string of text messages once the news spread. I had told my closest and bad news travels fast. I had texts off people back in England asking how I was. My parents were in absolute bits and just wanted me home.

If I'm honest I wanted to go home too. I didn't want to stay any longer. Sadly this was only the first day and I had a whole day tomorrow to get through.

"They better win that game," I thought to myself as I drifted off into a painful sleep.

"Are you coming out for the day? I'm waiting for you in the lobby."

It was match day and my mate had called me to see if I was coming along, I decided to go. I couldn't just sit in my depressing communist room. I was here and may as well just go to the game. Maybe things could still turn around and make the rest of the trip bearable. I'm not going to lie. I was in a lot of pain. Head pounding, constant sickness and blurry vision and every breathe I took cut like a knife across my ribs. I was no victim though.

I didn't want any pity. Sonia's look last night was enough. I was determined to not allow myself to be someone people felt sorry for. I had been in the wrong place at the wrong time. That's what I kept telling myself as I was getting ready to meet up with Ricky and head to the pub.

When I got down the lobby Ricky looked at me.

" Fucking hell - they got you good them Russians, eh?" He smiled and pat my back. I was glad he was joking around rather than giving me that look of pity I detested.

We took the metro to the pub. Some young Russian lads asked Ricky if he wanted to get a group together and meet up after the game to fight. We just laughed. This isn't football factory mate.

When I walked into the pub people turned around and looked at me, there was a split second where I thought they might treat me differently but the banter quickly resumed and the afternoon was OK. I ordered a Hooch and discovered that they were 9% in Russia. That should help with the pain for sure. Most of the familiar faces appeared during the afternoon. Perry was there with our mate Gary. We spoke a little bit about the night before and they told me about someone else they knew who had been beaten up. I felt relieved I wasn't the only one, as selfish as that may sound. Chess and Zeb joined us. Chess was mortified that despite making sure I was OK before leaving, I had somehow ended up in harm's way anyway. Just proves that some things can't be helped. I think everyone got the idea that I wasn't up for talking about what had happened so most of the chat was football focused. I never saw Sonia and her friends. I kept looking out for her every time the door opened but guess Moscow is large and the odds she would be in the same backstreet dig as us was low.

We all decided to leave for the stadium in a large group. Safety in numbers, a lad from Leeds declared. He was tall and of a larger build. He smelt of lager and lynx Africa.

"Stick with me and you be fine," he told me as we prepared to leave.

It was cold outside as we started walking down the road. No one said a thing until a lad in a tracksuit decided to pipe up and act hard. He belonged to the group of Leeds fans and looked like the kind of kid who had something to prove to his older peers. He belted out Rule Britannia once but it was more than enough. It had attracted unwanted attention and we were spat on walking down the street. All of a sudden a Russian came charging straight in with a punch, hitting my mate Kenny.
Kenny, who wasn't expecting that sort of attack, flew straight into the back of the rest of the English fans. They thought he was a Russian attacking them and started kicking him on the ground.

"I'm fucking English!" he yelled from the ground.

"Oh fuck mate I'm so sorry, it's bare chaos here," a lad apologised. We helped Kenny up and he muttered we should have taken a taxi instead. I thought to myself that I rather take my chances out on the street than getting into another taxi.

It was chaos with people kicking left right and centre. Not at all what it looks like on the TV when there's a fight. Chess grabbed my arm as if to say, come on lets scatter before we have to throw a punch or someone punches us. The Russian infiltrator was soon identified however, and let's just say the large Leeds lad dealt with him. I was tired at this point. My head was spinning and I was begging for some peace and quiet. The Leeds lot were all geared up now after that little brawl and was singing loudly as we walked into the metro station.

"This is insane," Chess exclaimed as we made our way inside the carriages. It was rammed inside and I remember spotting some Russians a few carriages down. No chance of fighting though as it was too rammed. You was lucky to be able to move your arm a centimetre. Swinging a punch was out of the question.

We got escorted off the metro by the police. I guess they were taking no more chances as the reports of several brawls from last night were coming in. I remember walking amongst all the other England fans and we all started singing. The Russians couldn't do a thing about it; we were completely shielded and in such a large group it would have been idiotic to attack us.

"Take that, you coward scum. You're quite alright to attack a girl who's alone but you can't do fuck all now we are all together " I thought to myself as we walked down the road to the stadium. I felt good for the first time since arriving here. The feeling of us against them was empowering.

That feeling didn't last for long however; as we turned round the corner the police disappeared and we were all of a sudden exposed and alone. The footsteps became faster and the singing quieter.

"It's going to kick off again isn't it," Chess sighed.

It never did thankfully, and we made it into the safe walls of the stadium. I don't remember that much from this game if I'm completely honest. I'm usually sharp when it comes to results. I can tell you who scored in what match minute in a game decades ago but this game was overpowered by my declining health. I do however painfully remember that we lost the game 2-1. It felt like the tip of the iceberg. A win after the ordeal we had was clearly too much to ask for. The doubts whether we would even qualify for the Euros was filling my head. A tournament without England? Surely not. Chess patted me on the back as we got up to leave.

I wanted to go home now. I wanted my bed and my mum and dad. I wasn't at all as tough as I thought I was. Little me wasn't at all ready to take on Russia. I knew that now.

They decided to let the English out first and keep the celebrating Russians in the stadium to avoid clashes. They put a Russian cartoon on the big screen and all the Russians was cheering and taunting us.

"Who the fuck celebrates a qualifying win by watching a cartoon?" I muttered to Chess and Zeb as we queued to get out of the stadium. It felt like forever, pretty much like everything else this trip.
When we finally got out, there was coaches lined up outside taking everyone back to their hotels. They were doing everything they could to avoid any clashes. I couldn't fault the Russian police. Shame their people was nothing like them. Much to my despair no coach was going back to my godforsaken hotel. Chess pulled me with him.

"Just come back to ours, I'll take you back later."

I sunk down on my seat on the coach. For being a coach full of football fans it was dead quiet. A few conversations between mates were heard but no general song or mischief. Me, Zeb and Chess said nothing. What was there to say at this stage? This trip was like all my nightmares in one.

When we got back to Chess's hotel everyone proceeded to drinking in the lobby. The police stood firmly outside the entrance and I suppose no one was going any pubs at this stage. I did some mingling and saw some familiar faces but I couldn't drink; I felt so sick at this point I could vomit at the thought of a beer. There were Russian girls from the nightclub downstairs walking around trying to get people to come with them. Last thing I needed right now was a naked Russian hooker, no offence.

All of a sudden there's commotion. Hundreds of Russians were outside surrounding the hotel trying to storm the lobby. The police were keeping them from getting in and I remember thinking " Here we fucking go again."

They never managed to get in but I think a few bottles flew inside. I went the toilet to vomit. The sight of my haggard face in the toilet mirror was scarier than the on-going attack outside. When I got back out someone told me we weren't allowed to leave; we were locked in for our own safety. These news were not well received by me at all. I just wanted to sleep until I could go home. My friend Lana offered to let me stay in their room. I had an early morning flight and felt a bit stressed as I would need to get back to my room and get my stuff before heading to the airport. It wouldn't surprise me if I missed my flight and got stuck in this place forever. Some nightmares never end. Chess assured me he would get up early to come with me and drop me to my hotel in the morning. Some heroes don't wear capes.

Lana and her friends were staying up for a bit so she let me into her room to sleep. I curled up in a little ball on the floor and drifted off to the background noise of the clamouring downstairs.

I woke up early to be sick again. Lana was fast asleep and I whispered thank you and left. I went down to reception and met Chess. We were both tired and fed up at this stage. He never said much back then but he's told me afterwards that it was the worst trip of his life and he had been so worried on that metro to come find me after I jumped out of the "taxi". He struggled to make out the stops in Russian and his phone kept ringing with the ring-tone " world in motion" basically broadcasting that he was British. I think our friendship was cemented that trip however. After that ordeal we were friends for life. He was my brother.

We got back to my hotel safely and checked out. The receptionist was the same woman who had dabbed my face two days ago. She didn't ask how I was or anything. The hospitality was zero. If trip advisor had been a thing back then I would have left them the most rotten review that's for sure.
I made it to the airport after another nervy taxi ride. Was this what it would be like from now on? Sheer panic as soon as I was in a taxi? At the airport the departure board was in Russian. Me and some lads tried to make sense of where to go. It was a never-ending guessing game that was not made any easier by the hostile attitude the airport

staff seemed to have towards us. I had battled a growing fear all morning that something else would go wrong and I would miss my flight and be stuck in Russia, so the second the flight took off I was overcome with relief.

" Good fucking bye," I thought to myself as I watched the city disappear beneath the clouds. Never again.

The flight was like a battlefield. Several people had cuts and bruises and the stories were circulating around the plane more frequently than the drink wagon. I heard a story about a man in a hostel who had his eye gauged out. I couldn't decide if I was lucky or unlucky.

"Are you that girl who got beaten up?" The voice came from the middle aged man next to me, and I suppose he had been waiting to ask me this since I sat down. My face wasn't exactly hiding what had happened. The cut on my cheek appeared to have gotten a bit infected and was oozing pus and blood from it as I had ran out of plasters. I nodded and he yelled across the aisle to his mates.

"This is the girl we heard about yesterday." They all came over and I found myself telling the story once again.

"Fucking cowards," they muttered in unison. "Wait until they visit Wembley next time."

"Did they cut your face like that?"

I replied that I don't think they cut my face, I think I scraped it when I hit the ground. At least that's what I was hoping happened. Seemed less dramatic.

I have had many moments of relief throughout my life but very few will beat the moment the taxi pulled up on my street back home and I saw my whole family in the window. I could of cried.

I was home. There had been moments during the trip where I had allowed myself to think that maybe I would never be home again, so to see them all there in the window was overwhelming.

After every trip I had been on we had always sat down together at the kitchen table and ate no matter what time it was, tonight was no different. The only thing different this time was the atmosphere. My usual enthusiastic stories had been replaced by a tired and beaten account of what had happened. My mum was emotional and my dad and brother were angry.

I was scared of going to sleep that night. I was scared that I would wake up in Russia and that me being back home was just a dream. I didn't sleep at all. Everything that had happened the past days were all of a sudden played up in front of my eyes like a bad movie. And it went on and on and on.

I was off work for two weeks after I got back. It turned out I had two broken ribs and a heavy concussion. I was told to rest in bed as much as I could. I don't really remember those weeks much; my dad was off work too and sat by my bedside like a hawk. He never said anything but I think he blamed himself for not coming with me to Russia. We went for walks now and then and life slowly resumed. Since coming back from Russia that evening I had not talked about it again. I had took all the bad things and locked them away in a little room far back in my mind. They tried sneak out and surprise me at night but I pushed them back. I didn't want pity. I didn't want to be known as the girl who got beaten up. Football was joy to me, and this past few weeks were trying to replace that joy with darkness. What happened in Russia meant nothing. It was just a series of unfortunate events and I wanted to move on. I did however make one promise to myself. Never ever again would I allow myself to be in a position where I was vulnerable again.

I returned to work a few weeks later. I was prepared for the pity to come flowing as usual. I lingered a bit by my desk that morning before I walked into the coffee room. I was determined not to let this become a sob story. I hated those. My colleagues looked up and before they even had a chance to say something I laughed and reached for a coffee mug.

"Don't worry, I'm OK. It only hurts when I cough."

Chapter 8
The move; welcome to England

Things were dark for a while after Russia. I felt angry. I didn't know where to aim that anger and so my nearest took a large part of it. This is not a sob story, so we won't go into too much detail. Let's just establish that I was not a very nice person the following year. I think my mum got the worst of it. My lovely, kind and patient mum who constantly appeared to be in the firing line of another one of my outbursts. I was anxious after Russia and even the idea of travelling made me shaky so I never made it over to England for their last qualifying game against Croatia. Which was probably for the best as England didn't qualify for the Euros. They lost the game 2-3, and my world was spiralling even further towards the bottom.

"Bet you regret wasting all that money and time off work when you didn't even qualify eh?" my co-worker said as we were sat at the desks waiting to go home.

I felt like saying something really rude back to him. Something about how whilst he sat at home on his sofa waiting for his wife to go to bed so he could watch porn I was jumping on a table in Macedonia leading the chants of the other fans. No money spent on football was ever a waste to me.

"Can't put a price on the memories really can you," I muttered and closed Auto-Cad down for the day. He shook his shoulders and left. He was so mind numbingly boring I was scared it would rub off on me eventually. I had started toying with the idea that maybe I didn't belong here. Don't get me wrong, I did actually enjoy my job, and me and my co-workers got on really well, but I felt like other things were calling me. I always told people I would move to England one day and be close to my football. They always laughed, presuming it was just one of those ideas I had but never acted on.

Maybe now was the time? I had messed up my education and as fun as it was to draw bicycle roads for the city council I think I needed more. After Russia I had been quite rude to many of my friends. Drink was involved and we all know alcohol and anger doesn't make you a lovely person to be around. I felt a need to start over somewhere else and there was never any doubt about where. The world was essentially my oyster and I could start again anywhere but my heart was in England. Probably always had been.
Every time I went over for football I fell more and more in love with its culture and people. I felt at home there.

"I'm going to move to England."

A moment of silence followed my announcement, and I think Mum was hoping I was just drunk and confused again.

I can't quite remember how the conversation went but Mum was worried, and rightly so. The past year had given her no confidence in my ability to cope alone. Dad was more practical. We went for a walk during our lunch break later on that week and he brought it up.

"I know you're going to do what you want, you always have. It's not going to be easy but you have our support. Your mum will come around to the idea."

We didn't really say much more about it. I was contemplating Sheffield and university to study PR, but changed my mind and went for Birmingham in the end. I knew more people there and some of them told me they might be able to help me get a job. It might have made more sense to move to Luton so I was close to my club football and not far away from Wembley, but I never really follow logic now do I? Besides, the train from Birmingham to London only took 1.5 hours which was a vast improvement on my current match day commute of 3 trains, a flight and 11 bags of crisps.

I went over to Birmingham in March 2008 and stayed at my friend Maggie's family's house for a week. She was the sort of girl everyone got on with, kind natured and organised. Her family made me feel at home instantly and we had family dinners together the first few evenings. It felt nice to be so welcomed.

The intention was to hunt for flats and jobs during my week there but it didn't go as planned. I was in a dark place and found myself being kicked out of Maggie's house after a very disruptive drunken night. I don't blame her mum one bit. I was really difficult to be around. I drank too much all the time and it put a massive strain on them, especially when they all had work the next day and I came back hammered in the middle of the night. I don't think I was being an arsehole on purpose. I'm actually quite kind natured deep down. It was like Russia had made me bitter, but I refused to acknowledge that it was because of what happened over there. If someone suggested I might be struggling because of Russia I would protest wildly. I didn't want to admit that it had affected me. It felt like I was giving in to it then. I didn't want to give that acknowledgement to such a horrible day. I didn't want it to be a chapter in my book. As you know it was and it was a big one but I never knew that back then. I thought I needed to put on a front. If you don't talk about it it's like it never happened right?

After I was kicked out of my friend's house I still had 4 days left in England until my flight home.
I remember walking down the streets of a Birmingham suburb with my suitcase thinking " What now?" I spent the day on a bench people watching. Despite the ordeal I still wanted to live here. Hard to explain why but it still felt like my future.

"Hey there, stranger."

I looked up and the sight of his face was enough to wash away a day of self-loathing.
You guessed right. Good old Chess drove from his home in London to Birmingham after finishing work and picked me up. We drove back down to London and I stayed at his for the weekend. It was just the break I needed. He went out with some mates of ours to watch football but I didn't feel like it; I hadn't been to a game since Russia. I spent the day at his watching TV and eating biscuits. I needed that alone time to figure out what I was doing with my life. Chess never judged me or even questioned what had happened at my friend's

house and I loved him for that. His ability to just accept people for who they were was a true blessing. I knew that with friends like that I would never be alone, no matter where I lived.

He dropped me back to the airport on the Sunday and I told him that the next time I'd see him I'd be living in England. He laughed.

" Maybe I'll come eat all of your biscuits, then."

Seeing as my attempt to view flats whilst over in England had failed I had to resort to more drastic measures. I viewed a flat online and asked my friend Laura to go view it in person for me. She lived around the corner and I knew her via friends from the football. She did and sent me some pictures. It wasn't how I had imagined my first home would look like but I decided to go for it. The only problem was that I had no job and they told me I had to pay a whole years rent upfront to guarantee tenancy. I had to turn to the bank of my father and lend a year's rent that I then agreed to pay him back monthly. Just like that I had exchanged paper work on a flat I'd never seen. It felt slightly surreal. I would spend hours on the estate agents website looking at the pictures of the flat and imagining myself in there. My best mates cried when I told them I was moving. Whether it was out of relief or sadness remains unsaid. I had packed all my stuff into a few suitcases and that was all I had. When I went to bed that last night in Sweden I remember thinking: tomorrow I will be going to sleep in my home in England. I was nervous but excited. I had this feeling that the next chapter of my life was about to start.

We couldn't just move over like normal people. We had to make it extra hard for ourselves, didn't we? Instead of flying over to Birmingham we flew to London to go to Wembley first. England was playing a friendly against USA. We were then taking a night coach from Wembley to Birmingham and would arrive at two in the morning. I had my mum, dad, brother and aunt with me and we all had luggage. They were going to stay with me for the first two weeks whilst I was settling in.

It was a rather stressful day. The London underground during lunch hour with loads of luggage is a test for the most patient person. We made it to the pub and my friend who arranges the coaches let us put our luggage in it. My aunt is not at all into football so she sat on the coach reading whilst we went football. It was a nice afternoon in the sun. Except from a Luton game where we got relegated earlier that spring, I hadn't been to any football since Russia. Most people hadn't seen me since and it was a jolly reunion. My mum and brother who were new to this lifestyle seemed to be enjoying it. Mum wasn't keen on the fact all the men took their tops off in the sun though. She probably didn't love all the songs we sang either, but I think she enjoyed seeing me happy again.

I felt proud showing off Wembley to my mum and brother who had never been. I wondered if they felt the same magic I did when you take those last few steps up and the whole pitch and stadium lays open in front of your eyes? England won 2-0 and it was time for night coach back. We had been travelling all day and was pretty tired by now but the rest of the coach was not. I smiled to myself as I watched my aunt's face when her sleep once again was interrupted by a rude song about tits.

We got to Shirley, where my flat was, around 2.30 am. It had started to rain and the streets were quiet bar the noise from our suitcases over the cobbles. The entrance to the flat was on a seedy backstreet and you had to go up a set of stairs to the door. We opened the door and a damp empty flat welcomed us. We had nothing quite literally so we wrapped up in bath towels and the odd sheet we brought and slept on the floor. I drifted off listening to the rain slowly dripping on my window and the distant noise of dads snoring from inside a wardrobe. Yes you read it right, dad slept inside a walk in wardrobe for 2 weeks.

The first two weeks went fast. We spent the days going to Ikea and Curry's to buy all the furniture and white goods I needed. The evenings were spent flat packing. We had no oven the first week and so the food had to be microwave meals from Iceland round the corner. It was far from a glamorous start to my residency, but I was happy. The Euros had started but I refused to watch it. If England weren't in it I didn't want to know. We had an old TV with really bad reception in the corner and dad would sit on a kitchen chair and try to watch football on it - but as soon as someone walked into the room the reception from the broken antenna would go. He would curse, and it was entertainment in itself to watch him.

The day my family was leaving to go back to Sweden eventually came around and it was hard. I had never lived anywhere except from my childhood room with my family. This was a big step from that comfort. I remember standing out on the back street to say goodbye. Everyone was crying, and my dad, who's always got it together, found it extremely hard to leave me and the wardrobe set-up behind. I stayed and watched them walk away. They were going back to what had been my home for 22 years but no longer was. I was sad about them leaving but I was not sad to be here. The 12 year old girl who had cried herself to sleep that night England lost to Argentina was finally home.

Chapter 9
Croatia; What's my wife going to say?

"Come on, you know you want to."

I was reading a text message from Zeb. It was about the South Africa 2010 qualifying campaign. We had drawn Croatia again and the schedule fell so that we were playing Andorra and Croatia away within a few days of each other. The idea to embark on a mega trip to Spain then to Croatia had started to take form in my head. I hadn't been to an England away game since last year. I missed it like you wouldn't believe. The Andorra game was to be played in Barcelona. Mum and dad was going to be on holiday down Calella outside of Barcelona at the time of the games so I worked out a really long advanced trip. Mum was no longer physically present but I couldn't almost hear her sigh through the email when I told her the plan.

I was going to fly to Barcelona and meet Dad. We were going to take the train down to the coast. I would stay with them for a few days. On match day me and dad would take the coach to and back from Barcelona. 2 days after I would travel from Barcelona to Germany. Spend the night there with my mate and we would then fly from Germany to Croatia and meet up with everyone for the game. Day after the game I would fly back to England via Germany. Mum told me the plan was enough to give her a headache but I had no qualms about it at all. I had been out of the game for far too long now.

"I'm in," I texted Zeb and we all went online to book our hotel for Croatia. Me, Chess and Lana were sharing a room and Zeb and our other mate Tommy were next door. I was working since a month back, and even though I now had bills to pay I was spending it on football yet again.

"Just make sure you aren't alone abroad at any point again," was how my mum ended her email. It sounded a bit paranoid but could you blame her?

"Azaaa, look it's your dad. He is sunbathing topless outside the airport!"

My mates were laughing and I was cursing. The observation was correct. We had just landed in Barcelona and my dad was waiting outside to take me down the coast for a few days. He had took his top off and was laying down on one of the decorative big rocks outside. His trademark white tennis socks and clogs combo was present too. I didn't feel like now was the time to display so much flesh but my dad did what he felt like always.

This was the first time I had seen my dear father since they left mine in June and it was now September, so I decided against moaning at him for the strip show he treated the airport arrivals to.
It was lovely to see mum as well and to spend a few days down the coast catching up. I also caught the sun very badly but that's a different story.

Me and Dad went into Barcelona early on match day to meet everyone. Despite it only being noon, most fans had gathered and took over the square already. I met up with Chess and Zeb and all the others and the drinking commenced. This was my first England away game since moving to England and it was almost as if everyone had forgotten where I was from originally. After years of always explaining why me and dad were there we didn't have to anymore. My dad was sat by the side of the square drinking with Jay and DL amongst others. Most of them hadn't seen him since Tallin 07. He also looked like he belonged there. He was not topless this time I may add.

No one had as much as mentioned you know what trip and it felt like things were finally back to normal. Zeb was leery and Chess was quietly confident. Some things never change I guess.

We met some of the absolute oldest football friends as well from Rosie McGee's and Geneva 05. It was good to see them and we lost track of time. Before we knew it we were late for the game. This was very unlike my dad who was practically born on time. He took me on some absolute stress journey to the stadium that ended in light jogging uphill. I could feel the beer jiggle inside my belly but my father looked unbothered, I was wondering at what point his top would come off.

We made it in the end but it wasn't without a few outbursts of despair for sure.

We had gotten rid of that utter mistake that was Steve McLaren and now had Fabio Capello instead.

We won the game 2-0 after Joe Cole scored twice within 5 minutes. Maybe not the most impressive performance but hey, it was better than loosing which we had become acclimatised to under Macca.

It was a late evening game so we had to take the coach straight back after. I said bye to everyone.

"See you in Zagreb on Tuesday!" Zeb shouted across the street before disappearing into the hustle and bustle of the night. His trademark match day striped top was soon swallowed up by a sea of other fans.

The coach back turned out to be a classic trip. We sat with some English people at the back singing songs, much to the locals' disapproval. There had been some arguments when boarding the coach; I think the Spanish had pushed in the queue and you don't do that with British people. Everyone knows that. Some strong words between locals and English had been exchanged. I won't repeat it. I think my son might be reading this.

I spent the next day resting on the beach before it was time to leave mum and dad behind yet again and embark on my solo trip to Croatia via Germany. I was tired. The combination of what I presumed was sunstroke and a hangover didn't sit well this balmy afternoon on a packed train to the airport. Slept on the flight and spilt a beer all over my lap. It looked like I had wet myself. When leaving the aircraft the air steward nodded at my crotch as to make me aware of the unforgiving stain. Thanks, I hadn't noticed.

"Long time no see, mate!"

Paddy's voice echoed through the arrival lounge in Cologne as I walked over to him. I couldn't remember when I had seen him last. All England games were starting to morph into one and I more than often found myself debating with my mates what happened where and when. We went straight out and it proved to be a wild night. We found a bar on a back street ran by a British man and it was empty except from me and Paddy. We drank the bar dry whilst blasting oasis and I vomited over what felt like the entire world. When I woke up on the floor of the low budget hotel room Paddy had booked I didn't exactly feel on top of the world. After a lot of grunting about how bright it is we made it onto our flight to Zagreb. After a beer on the flight I was starting to feel human again. Most of the mates had already landed in Zagreb and reports of sunny glorious weather were coming in.

They weren't wrong. I met up with Chess and we checked in, dropped bags and went out into the glorious sunshine of Zagreb. We had been warned ahead of this trip that it could be brawls etc. but it didn't feel hostile at all at this point. We walked down the street singing songs and the Croatian locals stopped and took pictures of us. In the evening we all settled into a bar area and stayed there for the night. We saw zero trouble but we had the police force present outside the pubs like a big thick barrier between us and the Croatians. Some Croatian fans from a pub across the road tried to heckle us, but it felt more like banter than hostile.

" Bit different to Russia eh?" Perry said as he sipped on his strange drink with whipped cream that he bought just because it was named shlag.
It was very different to Russia. This was helping me realise that Russia was a one off and not all trips were going to be like that. I looked at my mates as they poured beer into each other's trousers. No, not all trips were going to be like that at all.

"Ugh there's Pringles all over my clothes," Chess muttered as he woke up and noticed I had gone a bit wild with the snacks when getting back in last night. Lana wasn't flying in until today and we were meant to meet her in a bit. Chess shook his jumper over the bin whilst we discussed what we thought tonight's result was going to be.

"Probably get smashed again, eh," I said whilst zapping through the Croatian TV channels. They had on a special about how SMS bullying is not OK.

"Oh I don't know actually. I have a good feeling about today," Chess exclaimed. Maybe he was right. Hopefully he was right. We were just about to leave when Lana texted us. The airport had lost all her luggage and she had nothing. Stuff like this happened all the time and didn't faze us.

"Looks like we're off to do some shopping before the pub, eh?" I laughed to Chess as we took the elevator down the lobby.

" We'll need to top up the crisp supply as well" he muttered back.

Zeb and Tommy was already down the lobby drinking beer. There are absolutely no rules as to how early you can start drinking on match day.

"Oi oi," Zeb greeted us and Tommy who was hungover buried his face in his hands. Zeb never seemed down. Even in Russia when it kicked off he appeared to be full of glee. Having someone like that within your group was uplifting even during the hardest times. I had a lot of love for these lads I had come to know the past two years or so. In a very real sense they had become my brothers.
Especially Chess who had essentially saved my life more than once by now.

The day was pretty much like any other match days once we had got the shopping out of the way.
Sunshine, banter and beer. Unless you have been away with England you won't know the feeling of it all, but it's like a giant warm hug.

We stayed drinking in the bars as long as we could before we realised it was time to make our way to the stadium. It was a warm evening and we probably could have walked to the stadium but we left it a bit late so we jumped on the tram. The tram was packed with England fans and the singing started almost immediately; Zeb was of course in the middle of it all. What we didn't take into consideration was the Croatian lads down the front. As soon as the metro stopped at a station they all of a sudden shook a beer bottle so hard the top popped and flew off hitting someone in the face. They then jumped up and grabbed the handles by the ceiling, used them to swing and fly kick people straight in the face before cowardly running off the metro and onto the platform where they started hurling rocks into the tram. I heard someone shout duck and before I knew it a bottle narrowly missed my head.

More cries and someone was covered in blood. The doors had now shut and wouldn't open so one of my mates bent them open so the panicked people could get out. The Croatians were on the platform and there was a moment of commotion. Someone grabbed me and threw me against the back of the tram. It wasn't done in a nasty way. It was to protect me from the stream of bottles and things flying inside once again now the doors had been bent open. I looked around me and Zeb was still singing as if nothing had happened. I don't exactly know what happened next but the police arrived within minutes and for some reason arrested my two friends. This in itself seemed extremely unfair and loud protests broke out. One of the lads who was with us, Barry, had lost a tooth and blood was pouring down his face, got arrested too. Most likely only because it looked like he had been fighting.

We were all of a sudden reminded of the fact that you aren't completely safe anywhere; football rivalries are deep rooted, and we appeared to have acquired a very strong one with Croatia.

We made it for kick off just about and the atmosphere was electric. I looked down on my arm and realised I had someone else's blood splattered over it. Oh well.

It was warm and before I knew it most of the lads had flung their tops off and were chanting topless. Dad would of loved it. I wasn't going to follow suit. There was absolutely no need to scar people for life with that.

The game kicked off and what a game it was. Theo Walcott scored
after around 20 mins and we all exploded. And I mean absolutely
exploded. We jumped on top of each other and someone kneed me in
my throat. First half ended 0-1 and I was nervous. It would be
incredibly big to beat Croatia at their home. Walcott agreed and
netted again beginning of second half. Yet again things went wild,
we had only just about got back up from the floor when Rooney
scored our third. Whaaaaat? Was this actually happening? Were we
beating Croatia 0-3 away? Unbelievable.

Croatia scored 1-3 towards the end but Walcott shut it all down with
a hat trick and 1-4 minutes later.

"Didn't I say I had a good feeling about this?" Chess triumphed as
the game was blown off and we all jumped on top of each other for
the 5th time this evening. When we emerged back up from the pile
we were sweaty and happy. I had missed this feeling so much the
last year.

I glanced over at the pitch as we left. *Fuck, I love you*, I thought to
myself as we clapped the players on the way out.

This was a late kick off and it was just before midnight before we
came out of the stadium. The atmosphere seemed to have shifted. I
don't know why but we were walking back. Suppose we had had
enough of trams that day.

There was about 20 of us all walking in a little group. I wouldn't
have minded so much if it was a walk along main roads back to town
but it was not. We seemed to be walking down backstreets and it was
pitch black. All of a sudden a group of Croatians became visible
ahead of us. There was about 10 maybe even 15 of them stood at a
corner of a street. My mate Ade was leading the troupe.

"Heads down, not a fucking word," he said to us as we were
approaching their group.

I would lie if I said that my heart wasn't beating out of my chest. Those last few steps leading up to where they stood. The complete silence except for our foot-steps. The little flicker of a cigarette being lit. I swallowed as we were now walking past them just meters away.

I think we were all waiting for that moment when a brawl breaks out. Nothing happened. I think they were possibly waiting for us to attack them as much as we were expecting them to attack us. I don't know why they stood there appearing to be waiting but they didn't seem interested in trouble. They didn't even heckle us from a distance. Maybe they were involved in something else.

We started walking significantly faster after that.

"Fuck me, I fully thought it was going to kick off there then," Ade said as we approached the town centre and what felt like safe territory. No bars were open much to our dismay - seemed the Croatians had decided to close them all early to avoid trouble. We all went back and drank the hotel bar dry instead. Back inside we met up with the rest and got an update from our mates who had gotten arrested. They had been summoned to Croatian court the following day. It seemed to me like all they had done was to bend doors open to let panicked people out. The rocks and bottles came from the Croatians not us. We stayed up pretty much all night celebrating the 1-4 win. We went to a casino that was randomly open and caused havoc. At one point someone was drinking beer out of a trainer.

Chess passed out in bed and me Tommy and Zeb jumped on him. I can't remember falling asleep that night at all, it was just one big cheery blur and I'm sure Pringles crisps were involved yet again. The next morning the atmosphere down the lobby were slightly more subdued. It was time to head home and most people's heads were nursing big hangovers.

Before saying goodbye and heading to the airport we ran into Barry who had knocked out a tooth the night before. He was up in court later this morning. He told us about last night's ordeal and we agreed it seemed extremely unfair.

"See, I'm not even bothered about the court or the arrest or anything else ya know," he said as he was leaving through the revolving doors. "I only have one big problem. I'm coming back missing a fucking tooth. What's my wife going to say?"

Chapter 10
West World and umbrellas in Minsk

"I honestly don't get the appeal," said my friend whilst slurping the last bit of rum and coke from the bottom of her glass. It was Friday night and I was sat in the local pub across the street from my flat telling my friend about my upcoming trip.

"I don't know, it's just the rush of it all you know? It's the feeling of belonging somewhere. A home away from home."

" But you literally got beaten up! I just don't get how that's belonging." She looked at me and nodded to go to the bar.

I laughed and stood up. She gave me a tenner because it was her round, she was just too lazy to get up.

" Just because you've fallen off your bike once doesn't mean you're never going to ride it again does it?" I could feel her rolling her eyes at me as I walked off.

It was October and nearly a year since that trip to Russia. It had been a tough year for many reasons.
I had changed a lot. If you asked me I had toughened up a bit but if you asked my friends they would just tell you that I was overly aggressive.

England's last game this year was Belarus away and would be played in Minsk mid-October.
I was going and my mum was not happy.

"Belarus is technically Russia. I cannot believe you're going to a country like that again."

But she very well knew I always did what I wanted so no nagging in the world would keep me from going.

I had took extreme precautions this time. I had learnt from Russia's vital mistakes and booked a package trip my friend was organising. I would take a coach down to London and meet them all there and we would fly over together and there would be an organised coach at Minsk airport taking us all to the hotel, same when we were going home. I felt like I had covered all bases. This trip would involve no men in leather jackets and no women dabbing my face with vodka. I felt a bit bad going to Belarus as it coincided with my dad's autumn visit to England. He didn't fancy Minsk so he stayed at mine whilst I was away. I was only going for three days so we wouldn't miss too much time together. It was nice to once again have someone there to tell all your stories too when I got back as well. I had missed that after Croatia when I got back to an empty flat elated and full of stories. This time I would most likely be met by dad sleeping in my walk in wardrobe again.

I spent around 4 hours on a coach from Birmingham to Gatwick and it felt like it was stopping absolutely everywhere. My phone flashed with text messages from the likes of Zeb and Chess who were already there. I wish there was a way to fast forward all the travelling; there was nothing worse than the endless string of coaches, flights and trains you had to combine to get to where you wanted to be.

It was always worth it in the end though. Both for the football and for the memories. Memories of shutting down pubs, running from wild dogs, robbing off license stores and watching your dad dance to grease lightning in what I can only presume was a strip club. The strangers you met in pubs became family and the bond you shared over football was something else. You hated together but you also loved together.

I smiled to myself as the coach finally pulled into Gatwick. Another adventure was about to begin.
How could anyone even question why we loved this so much?

"For the love of god don't give him another drink."

We were all laughing as Paddy crawled around on the toilet floor in the pub. He had drinks all down his top and his speech was slurred.

It was match day in Minsk and everyone's mood was on top. Last night had been a laugh and I had woken up this morning with a loaf of bread in my bed. It was unclear why but I was past questioning at this point. I had met up with Dan in the morning, one of many close friends of mine throughout the years, and we walked to the pub together. I didn't think much of Minsk as a city; it was very worn down and the people were on the moody side, but hostility wise it was nothing like Russia. The journey yesterday had been problem free, the coach from the airport to the hotel felt like a lifetime but other than that, this trip had no similarities to a certain trip this time last year.

The hotel room looked like a prison cell but I wasn't planning on spending much time in there anyway so it didn't matter. It felt like absolutely everyone I knew was in Minsk. It was one of them trips that seemed to have attracted a lot of familiar faces. Paddy had made his way up from the floor and was now leaning on the cleaning lady who was surprisingly chirpy.

Harry started up " You've lost that loving feeling" and we all joined in. Soon the whole bar was singing along "Now it's gone gone gone woaaaaah" The locals walked past outside wondering why we were belting out songs by the Righteous Brothers. Not everything can be explained.

It was a late kick off, somewhere around 9.30, and temperatures had dropped to below freezing by the time we got into the stadium. Zeb was dressed as an extra from any shit hooligan movie ever made. I only had a t-shirt and a thin jacket. Chess was more sensible in a knitted cardigan. He always was. Some lads next to us were in those Russian fur hats and I wish I had thought about that.

It was a decent game if you could look past the fact we were losing toes to frost bites. England won 1-3 and it seemed like we were finally on course again after the debacle that was the McLaren era.

"We are absolutely banging in goals at the moment," Chess said as we made our way out of the stadium. It was around midnight and we were all headed back to the massive night club that was connected to our hotel. West World, it was called. We lost our souls in there that night, dancing and laughing and once again we were on top of the world. One by one familiar faces dropped in and soon the whole dance floor was exclusively English. We started chanting and soon " England til I die" was overpowering the club music. Chess managed to get himself in a drunken zone of absolutely no care in the world. We lost him for hours unless you count him dancing past us with an umbrella countless times. Chess wasn't the only one who was drunk, collectively we were a state. Zeb had drink spilt all over him, I was so sweaty from dancing my hair was standing straight up on my head, god knows how Chess felt in that cardigan of his. Paddy stormed the stage during a Belarus girls aloud act and tried grab the mic. DL was the only one not sweating as he appeared in a big thick scarf, most likely a gift of some Belarus sugar daddy he acquired on the sly. All in all it was a night to remember. On our way out there was some altercations with the law enforcement. Now, I had been exceptionally well behaved most of the trip in the sense that my aggressiveness had been kept at bay. Something was said that I didn't appreciate and for a second the more unpleasant side of me made itself known. I was lucky Gary and our other friend Nick were there. They somehow managed to diffuse the situation and avoid me being arrested in Belarus. That would of not been a great way to end a great trip and once again I owed a lot to my football brothers. When I woke up that morning I had a text from Gary.

"I saved you from Minsk jail last night Missy, next round is on you." I laughed to myself as I got up to get ready to leave. I had several other texts from the rest, most of them drunken drivel. Some of them about how Chess wouldn't stop his umbrella dance. I presumed he was in fact still dancing.
God I loved them all. Every single one of them. Imagine if I had never gotten into football? Imagine if my life had took a different turn and I had missed out on all this. My weekends would just be standard stories about how I got pissed in the local or how I won money on the Sunday bingo.

Instead I was sat on the window sill of a hotel in Minsk looking out over West World. It was empty now but last night it had been full of life. Just like us. Now we were about to return to the mundane reality of work again. The antics and stories would be locked up until next time.

Life felt good though. England were finally doing well after the dreadful 08 campaign and maybe we were finally on course for bigger things.

My phone flashed again as I was walking out the door. My mate summed the trip up with a single line text.

" West World has still got my soul.."

Chapter 11
Custody food is a dish best served cold

Christmas 08 was a messy affair. I think it was becoming more and more apparent that I wasn't doing as well as I was making out. On the surface I was living the dream. Moved to England and got my own place, worked within rehabilitation of addictions and mental health issues, something I loved doing. Money kept rolling in and was spent on football trips across the world. Not a lot seemed to be wrong unless you dug deeper and most people didn't. It gets uncomfortable if you start digging, doesn't it? It's easier to pretend everything is fine and so I did. Even during some pretty gloomy times leading up to Christmas I was still maintaining that things were fine. Me and Dad were planning the U21 Euros in Sweden the following summer and I was looking forward to that. The rest didn't really matter.

I was drinking a lot at this point but I don't think I thought that much about it. It seemed perfectly normal to drink as soon as you got back from work, alone or with friends. What else was there to do until the next football trip? My boyfriend at the time carried an immense weight and I don't think I ever did thank him for that. When I say that I wasn't a nice person I really mean that in every sense of the word. My intentions were good but they somehow got lost in the sea of alcohol and anger. I was a ticking bomb and it was only a matter of time before something would make me explode.

March 09 I was going to watch Aston Villa - Tottenham with Chess and the rest. They were coming up from London for an all dayer and I was meeting them in the pub beforehand. I wasn't supporting either of the clubs but any football is better than no football. We started early. My friend Josh picked me up at 10 and we went straight to the pub to meet the rest. It was a usual 3pm kick off and we had a rowdy day leading up to that. We were slamming back tequila like never before.

"Better than a day out with Luton eh," Chess laughed and I took a big swig of my beer. Luton was a sore subject at the moment. We were doing absolutely dreadful. Just thinking about them put me in a bad mood and I was already agitated when we got to the stadium. It was chaotic outside and the police presence was high. I was in a rowdy mood and found myself separated from my friends and with another group of big lads from Tottenham.

They were taunting the police and I joined in, I don't really know why. It's so easy to get dragged into situations in the spur of the moment. Bottles were flying from our side over to the Villa fans who were stood behind the police.

The police did all they could to keep the fans separated. Some of the Spurs lads attempted to break through the wall of the police and into the stadium but they were having none of it. They told us we aren't being let into the stadium as we were too rowdy and drunk, and all of a sudden there was a surge of bodies pushing from behind trying to get past the police. I struggled to stay on my feet and I'm sure I can still remember the smell of the Spurs fan's armpit as my face was forced straight into it. The police who seemingly had enough of all of us started to physically remove people from the group.

One of the lads were on the ground with a knee pressed against his back. He was spitting and swearing. I'm only little so there was no need to be forceful with me. I wasn't exactly presenting a threat to anyone, yet a large police officer felt the need to grab my arm and pull me with such force I flung to one side. That was enough for me. During that split second I felt him grab me I also felt Russia. I saw the man in the leather jacket smile. I felt the boots kick my ribs. I smelt the vodka. I finally lost it.

" Don't you fucking touch me!" I felt my fist hit him and that was enough. Within seconds I was on the floor wrestled down with such force I could taste the gravel; it tasted a lot like regret and bad decisions. I kept resisting and fighting back until I had to be restrained with handcuffs and chucked in the back of the police van. Russia had created a monster and that monster was finally about to face her biggest fear. Herself.

I woke up with a twitch. Where am I? I looked around the small cell. Yellow walls. Toilet in the corner. Mattress on a bench. Outside the big grey door I could hear someone repeatedly yell:
" Fucking pigs, you fucking little pigs." I was scared. I was fully aware of what had happened even though it felt blurry. The afternoon of tequila didn't help when I tried to get a clearer picture. I remember them taking my photo and finger prints when I got to the police station but other than that nothing. I must of slept for a good while to sober up as much as I had.

There was a sudden rattle and my door opened. A police officer with a blank expression handed me a pot of food and a spoon. I didn't know what to say. The waves of embarrassment made it impossible to talk at all. I stared down on the concrete floor hoping it would swallow me.

" Your solicitor will see you in a bit and prepare you for your interview later," he said in a monotone voice and the big grey door slammed shut. I stared at my food. Baked beans with wedges floating around in it. Solicitor? Exactly how much trouble was I actually in?

I poked about in my food and fished out the wedges. I didn't like baked beans and this version of them wasn't going to win me over. I was going through every emotion in the world. Most of it was regret. How on earth had I ended up here? What had I become?

I didn't get much time to ponder on that before there was another rattle of keys and the door once again flung open. A thin man with a forgettable face appeared in the door and introduced himself as my solicitor. He didn't look like the flashy solicitors I had seen on TV that's for sure. He looked like someone who gave you financial advice you didn't want to hear. He asked me to tell him what happened. I could only tell him the bits I remembered. When telling him I sounded like a brute. I was wondering if he thought I was one too.

" You could be looking at something like 6-12 months custodial for assault," he said as he took a seat on my elaborate bed set up. I swallowed. I couldn't process at all what he was saying. Prison sounded farfetched even in my world.

"But, I think we've got a good angle here. You're a young girl clearly caught up with the wrong crowd. You're lost, you drank too much, you felt intimidated. That's the angle you'll have to go with if you want to avoid time. It helps if you could cry," he said as he flicked through loads of documents in his binder. I didn't like it at all. I wasn't a victim and I didn't want to play one. I also didn't want to go to prison. I wouldn't last a second in there. I didn't belong there. He talked me through the process of the interview and asked if I felt ready. I didn't. How could I be ready? I had hit a police officer and was now told to try and put a sad angle on that. He left and said he would come back and get me when it was time for my interview. He was probably only gone for 10 minutes but to me that was the longest 10 minutes in my life. I had time to imagine myself in prison, and when they came to get me I was already eating prison food and smuggling cigarettes to inmates in my head.

The interview room was small and stuffy. The two police officers sat opposite me and my solicitor and there was a table with a recorder and a paper cup with water between us. They talked me through everything and I understood that I was going to be interviewed formally now. It would then be determined if I had to go to court and get my sentence handed to me there. They pressed the recorder and the interview started. My voice sounded so shaky I had to stop and take a deep breathe. I had never been in a situation where I felt so put on the spot before. The police officers were looking at me intensely and I felt as if everything I said came out in slow motion. It wasn't until I was given a chance to explain why this had happened that everything all of a sudden came over me at once. For the first time since Russia I was re-living it properly. I heard my own voice telling them about how I had been attacked and nothing had been right since. I told them about the nightmares and the constant stress whenever someone appeared to be a threat to me. I told them that I was angry with myself for being in that situation. It all came out and so did my tears. I'm sure my solicitor was rubbing his hands in delight at my tearful story. I had become a manifestation of everything I hated.

"I'm so sorry, I didn't mean for any if this to happen, I really didn't," I sobbed and looked down onto the table. I couldn't look them in the eyes anymore. I felt as if I was naked in front of them. I was so exposed. Everything I had convinced myself didn't matter for two years was now on the table for everyone to see and it wasn't a pretty sight. I hated that I didn't even have to put on a performance as my solicitor so eloquently called it. My life really was this pitiful.

It was quickly established that I wasn't a criminal. Nor was I out to cause trouble. I was just a lost girl with issues that needed dealing with. It was determined that it wouldn't be beneficial for me to serve time. I drew a sigh of relief; no prison thank god. I was going to be given a caution for assault but this caution had conditions. I had to give up my football membership and I had to go and talk to someone about my drinking and try and work through my issues. I agreed and nodded to everything, I was so tired and drained at this point I had no fight left in me.

"Congratulations, you've really gotten off lightly here. Make sure you don't repeat these mistakes, people aren't as understanding of repeat offenders," my solicitor said as he shook my hand and walked away down the corridor. It didn't feel like a congratulation was fitting. Sure, I had narrowly escaped serving time but what else was there to cheer for? Look at the utter mess I had made of my life the past two years. Look how I had allowed myself to become the victim I swore I wasn't going to become. It wasn't Russia that was holding me back it was me and my complete inability to help myself rather than trip myself up.

I had lost concept of time but by the time they let me out and gave me my belongings it was four in the morning and a new day was dawning. I had been in the cell over 12 hours. I felt a massive wave of relief when I got in the taxi and we started making our way back home through the night. I had feared I wouldn't get to go home in a long, long time. I knew that this had to mark a massive change in my life. I couldn't go on as I had for the past two years. The fact they had took my membership and I now had to wait for the FA to send me a letter with a banning order was something I hadn't even had time to process yet. Maybe I didn't want to. The idea of a life without football scared me almost as much as a prison sentence; in fact, it was a sentence in itself. Football had been my life for the past 10 years and I didn't know who I was without it.

"I guess I'm about to find that out now," I thought to myself as I closed the front door behind me.

Chapter 12
U21 Euro 09 – Mark Noble is number one

"Does it say for how long you're banned?" Chess asked when I texted him to let him know my banning order had arrived. It didn't. It didn't specify anything, which made the uncertainty worse. It was just signed by crowd control adviser Bill Hopkins, whoever that was. I needed to know that I could re-instate my membership one day. I had to know that my football would come back. It couldn't end here. My other friend who had been banned told me it's usually 10 years or less. He had been able to re-instate his after 10 years no questions asked. A decade seemed a long time. It was the same amount of time that had passed since that summer I fell in love with football. My friends convinced me I would still be able to get the odd ticket here and there for games. I still had the U21 euros in Sweden booked and no banning order in the world could keep me from that. Me, Zeb and our mate Andy were flying from London to Gothenburg and then onto a coach to the small city of Halmstad where dad would meet us and we played our first game against Finland. Some people were laughing at us for going to an U21 tournament and said it wasn't the real deal, but this was tomorrow's England and as I've said so many times before: any football is better than no football, especially now when it had essentially been taken away from me.

It was a long journey. Zeb kept us busy with his football guessing games the whole coach ride.
" Name a footballer that starts with an A and then I name a footballer that starts with the last letter of the footballer you just mentioned, get it?" I loved Zeb; his constant enthusiasm had kept us going many times before and this journey was no different. We met up with Dad and walked to the accommodation. For some reason he wasn't greeting us topless this time and for some reason that felt like a disappointment. The place where we were staying wasn't a hotel but

a terrace of rooms all joined together with a lawn in-between. Some finish guys had already arrived and they seemed friendly enough. There was no bars as such in the area so we found an outdoor cafe with live music and settled down for the evening.

It was match day tomorrow and the night before looked a lot different to the usual night before. At least I was back doing what I loved. No one had mentioned the arrest yet and I think it was to become one of them subjects no one wanted to bring up, that included myself.

"Mark Noble is number one!" Our song was echoing across the narrow streets of Halmstad as we were walking into town for pre match drinking. It was lovely and warm and everyone was in a good mood. Dad had insisted on us walking and we didn't mind, we had plenty of booze for the walk. They had set up a little fan area in a big marque in the town centre so we went there. Met up with some other Englishmen and the afternoon flew by drinking and laughing. I had missed this. The game was played at Orjans Vall, my dad's Swedish club team's home stadium, so he was beyond nostalgic as we walked into it. We didn't have tickets next to Zeb and Andy so arranged to meet up straight after. Me and dad had got our tickets outside of England fans so we were stood with the Finnish fans which proved to be a difficult test.

England went 1-0 up and we cheered loudly amongst all the Finnish fans, which didn't go home very well. Finland got a penalty and scored. The Finnish went wild in the stand which I can understand but this large woman then turn around and start jumping up and down and waving her hands in my face cheering at me and laughing. I could smell her breath she was that close. Unacceptable behaviour if you ask me, so I slapped her across her cheek. Her boyfriend quickly came to her rescue and commotion broke out in the stand. My dad was quick to deal with the boyfriend and by the time the guards came over to calm things down both me and dad played it cool whilst the woman was frothing out of her mouth like a caged dog.

"She waved and pointed in my daughters face so she pushed her away that's all," my dad said innocently to the security guard and looked at the wild woman as if to say " Can you blame us?"

"That's not true, she hit me," yelled the woman, her face bright red and blotchy. She was extremely agitated and aggressive whilst me and dad calmly just reassured them that all we are interested in is the game and the guards believed us over them.

They told us all to keep our distance and if there was more disruption we would all be chucked out and then they walked off. I winked at dad and he smiled. The woman turned around to say something but my dad quickly caught her.

" If you as much as turn around to my daughter one more time it'll be the last thing you'll ever do."
She didn't move for the rest of the half.

I laughed to myself; aggressive behaviour during sport truly ran in the family. It was a good game and some Finnish man streaked as well which was memorable.

England won the game 2-1 and you can imagine how much we celebrated when Richards scored. Not in her face, however, we're not childish like that. After the game we met up with Zeb and Andy and proceeded to walk into town. They said they had seen some commotion over at our stand and my dad laughed.

" Oh that? That was just Az slapping a Finnish lady across the face, you should of heard the sound it made."

Zeb and Andy wasn't staying for the whole tournament like we were so we only had the weekend with them. It involved many memorable memories including an underground bowling alley that was also a nightclub; and in true Zeb style they overslept the morning they were going back and missed the coach to Gothenburg. They ended up having to pay for a taxi the whole way to Gothenburg instead. It was easily over 250 pounds. We laugh at it now but they didn't laugh back then that's for sure.

Me and Dad took a coach to Gothenburg for England's game against Spain and they won 2-0. We got back early morning after a long trip and the accommodation had been completely trashed. We looked at each other in confusion but got an explanation the next day. A whole bunch of Swedes had arrived for the midsummer celebrations and trashed everything. My brother also arrived that afternoon to join us for England's final group game against Germany. He didn't trash anything though. It was great to spend some days down the coast with my dad and brother and I already felt more at peace with things. The only thing that wasn't peaceful was the Swedes at our accommodation. People talk about badly behaved Brits abroad but having been with both I can confirm that the Swedes at home took the price. I don't mind rowdy behaviour as you know but this wasn't that. It was just pure childish behaviour, repeatedly chucking a chair against our door all night. Dad keyed their cars in the morning when leaving for the game. My dad lived in a world where zero fucks given was a main theme. Me and my brother just laughed. We had grew up with him, this was nothing odd at all.

England and Germany ended 1-1 and were through to the semi- final against Sweden. We decided that it was a game that was best watched at home away from any trouble and possible clashes. I certainly knew my limitations by now. We went back to Mum and Dad's house to spend some time there catching up with friends and family.

In true Sweden – England style the game ended 3-3 after we had been 3-0 up and we were now dreading penalties. Me and dad had tickets for the euro final in Malmo 3 days later. England don't win penalty shoot outs, as we know, so we had little hope as usual. England won this time however and we all exploded in a pile on the floor. My dad got delirious and wrote off the 10 grand debt I owed him for the rent he paid upfront. It seemed I had many things to celebrate that evening.

"I'm actually a little bit nervous," I said to Dad as we walked into the stadium for the final against Germany. Sure it was " only" the U21 but still. We had lived and breathed this tournament the past two weeks. It hadn't been anything like Germany in the sense there was not many fans around to meet up and drink with but it had nonetheless been a great few weeks filled with live football. Just what I needed. There was never a time when football wasn't what I needed.

It wasn't the end that we would have hoped for, however. England got absolutely annihilated and lost 4-0. Me and Dad didn't say a thing on the long walk back. It was like it always was when we lost something. Silence. I felt bitter. Winning the U21 euros would have been massive for our football but we had to get humiliated in the final. I was worried this would be my last game in a long time. I had a sinking feeling when we got back to the hotel that night. As I sat on the window sill watching the world pass by I could hear dad stress eating crisp bread. For a second it felt like we were back in the old apartment in Germany 06. I smiled in the middle of all misery and wondered if he had some apple wine back there too?

I said bye to my dad in Malmo the next day. It felt weird having been together at the football for so long but not return home together. I wasn't overly excited to get back to my empty flat in that sense. I knew I had a lot of shit to deal with now and it seemed like a long road ahead.

On the train from Malmo to Copenhagen I met a gentleman in a suit and FA badge. I was sat sulking by the exit and as I was wearing my football top he presumed I had been to the Euros.
We spoke briefly and I told him I had been over for the whole tournament. He laughed and gave me a sticker from the FA.

"We sure need more loyal supporters like you, keep it up."

As he turned around to exit the train I caught a glimpse of his name badge I hadn't seen it before as the fold of his suit jacket covered it.

"Bill Hopkins."

I laughed to myself. The irony of the man who had written my banning order letter also telling me they needed more supporters like me was just too much.

"I'll be sure to keep that in mind, mate," I replied as he walked off the train and onto the platform.

I watched him as the train pulled away from the station. I put my headphones back in and closed my eyes. For the first time in 4 years I had no football trip booked ahead. I didn't know what was around the corner and I didn't know when I would be at a game again. I knew one thing though: my hiatus from football was about to start here, on a sweaty train back from a tournament and with Bill Hopkin's sticker firmly on my top.

Chapter 13
Absence makes the heart grow fonder and the wallet bigger

"Don't allow Russia to keep you hostage," said the therapist as I got up to leave. I looked at him. He was roughly my age and I found it really hard to take anything he said serious when I was sure he spent his weekends sniffed off his head in some night club. I didn't like him very much and he knew that. I disregarded everything he said and we weren't getting anywhere. I didn't want to be here but it was better than prison. He wanted to talk about feelings and emotions and I didn't.

I felt relatively alright. I knew I had been drinking and carrying a lot of built up anger for a few years now, but I was dealing with it in my own way. I didn't need James the therapist to tell me what to do. He wanted to find problems in areas where there weren't any. My relationship, my family, my friendships. I found that extremely intrusive and if anything, seeing him weekly made me angrier.
I had tried explain to him again and again how my childhood was happy, it had no so called triggers at all. There was nothing in my childhood that 15 years later made me punch a police officer at football. He had read far too much Freud, bless him.
It was simple. Something happened to me recently and instead of dealing with it I drank and lashed out a lot. There you go. Problem solved. The arrest six months back had been a wake-up call in itself and I was drinking far less now. My work was going well and the only thing missing was the football; otherwise things were looking good. I still panicked now and then in taxis and that feeling would come creeping back, but compared to how things had felt for a while this was minor. I didn't see the leather jacket taxi driver in my dreams so much anymore, I didn't hear the music from his car at night either. I didn't feel angry, not even at myself for burying my head in the sand. Everyone has their own coping mechanisms. I think the image of me restrained on the ground outside a football stadium like an angry dog had been enough to slap me back into

reality. I didn't want to be that person anymore

"See you next week," James said as I walked out the door. I didn't. I contacted the agency and requested a different therapist. What's the point going to see someone and talk about your anger when all you want to do is punch the person who's helping you?

I saw James out a few months later when I was in a pub celebrating my friend's birthday. He was leaning on a table alone, glazed look on his face whilst trying to put coins back into his pocket. I didn't say hello but he saw me when I walked past to leave. Freud was nowhere to be seen anymore.

Life without football went on. I was focusing on other things, work, friends and getting myself back on track. I was still working within mental health which I really enjoyed. I was in a relationship with Josh and things were pretty peaceful. This all changed one grey November afternoon.

Me and Josh went to Tesco to get dinner stuff. I had been sick a few days back and had absolutely no energy so I got a pregnancy test when Josh wasn't looking. We had only been together 9 months and I didn't want to worry him with any pregnancy scares. I always thought I was pregnant so there was no need to raise any alarms yet. Most of the time I just felt bloated and nauseous from eating too many custard slices, sad but true. He proceeded to start with dinner whilst I jumped in the shower.

I took the test without as much as thinking about the possibility of two lines. It wasn't until I glanced at it whilst getting into the shower that I saw just that. Two pink lines staring back at me.

I went into the shower and just started crying. I wasn't ready for this. Me as a mother? Someone calling me their mum. Oh no, I was far from ready for this. I had time to think thousands of horror scenarios before I finally stepped out of the shower. I didn't even get dressed but wrapped myself in my towel and ran down the stairs. Josh was sat on the sofa flicking through the channels for something to watch. Would most likely settle for Grand Designs.

"I'm pregnant..."

My shaky hands were holding the pregnancy test up in-front of a puzzled Josh.

" How? You're on the pill aren't you?

I nodded slowly. A moment of panic followed. The dinner on the hob boiled over, along with my emotions. We had a long talk and after a lot of back and forth we decided that this was a good thing. We both had settled jobs, I had a void to fill after the football ban and in terms of staying off the drink, this was as good a reason as I ever would have. My doubts and fears of being a mother slowly faded the next few months as I was preparing for the birth of what we had found out would be a little boy. I almost instantly saw myself along-side my son at the football.
It's strange how things just tend to work out for themselves. I felt lost after the football ban and I didn't really knew who I was if I wasn't at the games or talking about the games or thinking about the games. Now I had another much bigger role to take one. The one of a mother. I really couldn't wait to welcome my son to the world.

I'm going to fast forward a little bit. Otherwise you'll end up ploughing through pregnancy, childbirth and terrible twos and there's already plenty of those books around. I had Freddy in July 2010 just after I turned 24. It was love at first sight like nothing else ever before. Not even Beckhams freekick 2001 against Greece could compare although obviously very close second.

Two years later Josh asked me to marry him on top of the empire state building. I was on top of the world, literally. Our daughter, Mia, was born the year after and the family was now complete. Did I miss the football? Of course I fucking did. Every tournament that I wasn't at felt weird. I was still very much in touch with all my football friends and they would text me from the tournaments and I would feel that little stab in the side of my chest. An ache to be back there. Drinking in pubs all night, jumping in fountains or scrapping at football games seemed so distant now when my day consisted of nappy changes and tantrums. I do genuinely believe that every stage in life has a purpose however, and after 10 years of football I needed this down time to recharge.

I never considered the door to the football shut. I lived my life knowing that I will be back one day. I will once again stand next to my best mates and belt out the national anthem and feel that certain feeling only football can evoke. I would be back.

Me and Josh broke up the engagement 4 months before the wedding. It genuinely wasn't an ugly but a rather dignified time of our lives. We had been through so much and sometimes it makes you stronger but other times it breaks you. We grew in two different directions. The last year together was like we had shared custody already. We didn't spend any weekends together. If he was out I stayed in with the kids and vice versa. I think we met at a time when my life was turmoil and we grew around that. When I got out of that darkness it seemed like we wanted different things and we ended up growing apart rather than together. There was no bitterness at all the night we broke up. It was like we were watching a movie and we both knew it was coming to an end. We had our dinner and after we had watched the standard soaps he turned off the TV. There was a sudden silence in the room as he turned around to me from his spot on the sofa.

"So are we going to talk about this then?" he said in a hesitant tone that didn't feel familiar.

I knew what was to follow but when he said it, it still felt foreign. We explored all our options very carefully the following hours. Was there any way this could be saved? In the end we both agreed that there wasn't. We weren't happy together and we didn't want to raise kids in that environment. If the last year of our relationship had been hard, the break up was easy. We went to bed that night with a sense of relief. I was scared, of course. The idea of being a single mum with two kids and a full time job was daunting but it wasn't exactly an unheard of situation and I would be fine, just like I had with everything so far.

I moved out of the house and into an apartment shortly after we broke up. As it was an amicable break we remained very good friends determined to still raise the kids together. Most people expected me to go off the rails after such a big break up but I never did, and I think it was at that point I realised that I had finally grown up. We shared the custody between us. The kids took it quite well. It's amazing how quick kids can adapt when you go about it the right way. I tried to take a leaf out of their book as I had always struggled immensely with changes.

Was it awful when the kids were at their dads and I was alone again? Absolutely. I would cry every time I dropped them off. That's life though; it's never perfect and it's not meant to be. It's full of compromises and lessons. All the time to myself really made me accept my own company again and I became a better person for it. When I had the kids I was a fully focused mum; when they were at their dad's I spent time recharging my batteries, I found a balance eventually and so did the kids.

It's wrong to call it a broken home. There's nothing broken about realising that two parents work better separately than together.

The year that followed after the separation wasn't easy but it taught me so much and I grew so much closer to my children. It was the three of us against the world. Mia was this fierce yet super cuddly little girl who enjoyed dancing and writing. Freddy had grew up to become a witty and sharp lad with a glowing passion for football. What about following England? Surely with more free time and a stable job it would soon be time to return? That old itch of wanting to go to games was once again flaring up and this time the itch needed to be scratched. I just had to figure out when and how. It was possible for me to get tickets without being a member. I would just need a member to sort it for me which they all gladly helped with.

It was about a year later, in 2016, when Freddy started nagging at me about going to football. His persistence reminded me of myself when I started pestering my dad to join in 11 years back. Imagine if he had said no? Maybe my life would have taken a completely different turn. I never would've got the bug and eventually moved to England. Never would have had the memories I did and Freddy and Mia wouldn't exist. It felt like maybe Freddy's journey was about to start now.

He was 6 years old and had followed euro 2016 passionately with me on the TV (Fuck you Iceland). The qualifiers for 2018 world cup was about to commence and we had a game against Malta at Wembley in October. Josh was hesitant.

"Do you really want to start this whole thing up now and have him wanting to go to all games like you did?"

I'm not sure why people persistently considered my years of following England as something bad. It made me as a person and I wouldn't swap the memories for anything in the world. If I could give Freddy the same chance of that sense of euphoria and belonging, why wouldn't I?
I asked my mate Gary to sort tickets out for us through his membership that same afternoon and the second I picked Freddy up from school I smiled.
"We're going to Wembley, son. It's time to return."

Chapter 14
The return

"Look Freddy, there it is, the arch on Wembley!"

Freddy looked out of the window. His little face lit up with
excitement. We had taken a coach to Wembley and he had chatted
the whole way. He reminded me of a young Zeb the way he insisted
on playing number games and football player games. I felt a surge
of excitement washing over myself. It had been 8 years now since I
last went a game at Wembley, yet it felt like I had never been gone.
The messages were flooding in about what pubs people were going
to. We didn't have that much time after the coach arrived sadly, but it
was more than enough to pop up to the Torch and meet some of the
usual suspects. We got off the coach and started walking down
Wembley way towards the pub. A big bunch of Malta fans jumped
up in-front of us and started singing and dancing " welcome to
Malta."

I looked at Freddy. He was not the slightest intimidated, instead he
smiled at me. I knew that smile all too well. It was the same smile I
would give my dad throughout the years in various situations. It
meant something special I knew that much. Last time me and my
dad had done it was after we tricked the security guards into
believing we had done nothing wrong the time I slapped the Finnish
woman. I hoped me and Freddy would come to share that sense of
always having each other's backs too, maybe just in a little bit less
violent circumstances. His sister Mia was too young to go any sports
events yet and she was mostly interested in dance. I often thought
about her with a little bit of guilt whenever me and Freddy did
something football related. I hoped she would grow up to develop
her own interests I could follow. I could probably write another
whole novel just on the subject of mom guilt.

We got to the pub and although it was rammed, my friends weren't
there yet. Me and Freddy went the bar and it didn't take long before I
heard the familiar sound of DL's voice echoing across the bar.

"Bazza, me duck!" he exclaimed before picking me up in an embrace. Freddy watched on as we fell into a daze of nostalgia; reminiscing about Macedonia and being chased by wild dogs, all the countless times he hit on fathers instead of their daughters and of course West World. Freddy's eyes were flickering with delight. All these stories about his mum he had never heard before. Up until this point I had just been his boring mum telling him to wash his hands and brush his teeth. Now I was this walking legend full of stories from a gone time. I was touched when I watched my mates from the old days pick up my son and joke with him like we had joked back in the days. It's funny with the football, you can be gone for years yet nothing will have changed when you return. It was like a safety net that was always there, no matter what. I was wondering if Freddy would grow up to take his son or daughter to games and feel the same nostalgia as me?

We said bye to our friends and made our way to Wembley. It was late afternoon and a crisp chill in the air as we walked down the road. I was soaking up every bit of it. The distant clamouring of voices. The children laughing. The smell of burgers from the countless burger vans along Wembley way. Then out of nowhere it's just there in front of you. Good old Wembley in all its glory.

"It's huge mum!" Freddy exclaimed. He didn't seem at all put off by the massive crowds and being so small. I grabbed his hand.

"You've got to stick with me now, buddy." I wasn't used to having any responsibility at football games. Usually I would hang in the pub until the last minute then leg it down the road to make it for the national anthem. This was different, however. I wanted to make sure Freddy had the best possible experience and that didn't involve a sweaty run and elbowing people at turnstiles. The second you become a parent your priorities shift and the football was no different. I didn't mind at all though. In a sense I think having Freddy with me kept me out of trouble.

We were finally approaching the final steps leading up to the stands. I knew what was to come. I knew the feeling of taking the last few steps and having Wembley open up in-front of your eyes. A feeling of being so small yet so included. Say what you want about football; unless you're part of it you'll never quite understand. Understand that feeling of having Wembley open up in front of your eyes.

I turned to Freddy.

"Isn't she beautiful?"

He nodded and then he smiled that smile again. I knew he felt it too.

England won 2-0 and Freddy was absolutely bitten. He sang along to the songs and made most of the people around us smile at his extensive knowledge about players and statistics. It was a special feeling when England scored and I got to pick my son up and cheer like my dad had with me so many times in the past. I really was nostalgic this evening. I never saw Chess and Zeb in the end as they got delayed on the tube and we had to leave the pub, but we reassured each other there was always next time because that's what it was like. There was always a next time. It didn't matter if I got beaten up in Russia or if Kenny accidentally took a beating by his own. There would always be a next time. Barry who lost a tooth in Croatia was back the next game - what his wife said wasn't part of the story, but he was still there. Life changed as we grew up but the football remained a solid focal point. I had gone from rowdy teenager to a responsible mum, yet the football games felt the same.

I looked at Freddy as he was falling asleep on my lap on the coach back. His journey was only just beginning, and if it was to be anywhere near as eventful as mine he better get ready to buckle up. As the coach pulled into Birmingham coach station Freddy woke up. He still had his little England flag firmly in his hand from Wembley. As we stumbled off the coach sleepy and aching for bed he looked at me.

" When's the next game, mum?"

Chapter 15
What about Bulgaria?

"But mum we have to go to an away game now, it's time!"

I looked at Freddy where he sat on the floor in his room sorting out football tickets and reminiscing over past games we been to. It was summer 2019 and the past few years had been good to us. Freddy had been back to Wembley a few more times and now had the same soft spot for it as I had. He was playing football himself and was also a season ticket holder at Birmingham City; to say football was his life was an understatement. Mia was into cheerleading and gymnastics and we had been to see her compete a few times. She had no interest in football which I suppose could be seen as a blessing as it was costing me a fortune already with Freddy. She had however convinced me to buy her a Luton town top just because she was adamant she was supporting the same club as her mum. When Freddy wore his blues kit she would wear the Luton top and it would raise a few eyebrows around various places we visited that summer, much to Freddy's bemusement.

It was now 10 years since I was arrested and banned and I had took a gamble and re-applied during the summer. It had come back successful and I was once again part of the England fans travel club. They did a background check when I applied so I presume the caution I had for assault had been spent. Freddy joined too and I think we both knew it was soon time for his first away game. We already had a trip to Wembley booked in November for the last game of the euro 2020 qualifying campaign.

"What about Bulgaria away in October?" he said, and looked at me, almost prepared for me to laugh and say 'no way mate' as I had to most of his wild suggestions.

I thought about it for a second. Was it doable? Would it be safe for me to take a 9 year old kid to an England away game already? What would his dad say about him missing school? As new members our caps weren't enough to get tickets for away games yet, so could we get tickets elsewhere?

"Possibly," I replied and instantly regretted it as he flew up from the floor in jittery excitement.

"Really? Can we really go to Bulgaria?"

"I don't know yet, mate - let me check with my friends to see if anyone on high caps have spare tickets." I knew that Freddy was just like me and even though he was significantly younger than I was when I started going to football, I knew that he wouldn't take no for an answer. If he got it in his head that he wanted something he would make it happen. It's not a bad quality but as a parent it can be endless. I suppose my dad felt that way about me when I dragged him on countless trips across Europe sleeping on various floors and benches. If you asked him though he wouldn't want it any other way and neither would I. Football had both shaped and changed my life and those memories was not something I would swap for any fortune in the world.

I asked around amongst my friends and it turned out that Lana would be in Bulgaria but not actually going to the game, and she said me and Freddy could buy her tickets off her. I looked up hotels and found a lovely one in the middle of the town. Flights were relatively easy, a transfer in Frankfurt and then onto Sofia. I hesitated a bit before I took any decisions. It wasn't that common that kids tagged along to away games, and I didn't want to take him unless I felt it was safe. I spoke to Perry and he assured me we would all stick together. Chess wasn't going to this one and Zeb would be in Sofia the day of the game like Lana but not actually going to the game. They were all going to Prague on the Saturday for England's game against Czech Republic then flying straight to Sofia, spend the day with everyone and fly back home during the game. My hesitation was soon gone at just the idea of being able to introduce my football mad son to the phenomenon that was away days. It was nothing like the home games. It was hard to explain what it was. I guess the age old cliché of " you'd have to be there" was true in this case.

I booked flights, hotel and sorted tickets with Lana that same afternoon whilst Freddy was in his room, clueless as to what was going on. His birthday was coming up and what better present to give than Bulgaria away?

As expected, Freddy was absolutely out of his mind with excitement when I gave him the present. He was telling all his team mates about how him and his mum were going to Sofia to watch England. I was equally excited; this was the real return to football. Sure, we had a soft spot for Wembley but it couldn't be compared to away trips. I had not been to an away trip since the glorious trip to Minsk 11 years earlier. My life had been mainly work and parenthood which I dearly loved but it was time to bring football back for real.

Freddy's father was unusually nervous about the trip. I guess he knew exactly what I used to be like during away days with England. I tried to assure him that I would rather die myself than letting Freddy end up in harms way but that did nothing to calm him. Bulgaria had been outed lately for extreme racism. They had an apparent violent fan base according to the news rags, who loved it when they got to write about people behaving badly at football. To them, football fans were the lowest on the social scale, a bunch of uneducated brutes who only went abroad to drink beer, smash people's heads in and wolf whistle at women. I had seen them at times and I had been them at times, I would lie if I said otherwise, but the football scene was by no means dominated by that category. Most of the people I had met through football was smart people with good jobs and families who happened to love following their football across the world. I was certain I would be able to keep my Freddy safe.

The night before the trip his dad sent me a newspaper article about football violence and riots in Prague during the weekend, allegedly caused by England. I text my mates who were there and none of them had seen any trouble at all. If you're looking for trouble you'll find it, just like anywhere in life. This was not exclusive to football by no means.

"You better be able to keep him safe. I'm not very happy about this," his dad said. It was unlike him to ever stress about things and it made me question if I had taken on too much. We had to be up at 4am the following morning for our 6am flight, so Freddy went to bed early. He was a bundle of excitement when putting his Birmingham city tracksuit out on his chair ready for the morning.

I struggled to fall asleep that night. My mind was flooded with a mix of absolute joy to be back and a slight concern that things once again would go wrong. I had said to friends and family many times before that things wouldn't go wrong and they did. I had took every precaution though. I had the number for the most legit taxi firm in my phone, I was meeting Perry and his friends at the airport and taking the same flight and we would make our way from the airport to town together. There was little room for anything remotely Russia-like. I closed my eyes and slowly drifted off. My dreams that night was a mix of panic in taxis and elation at winning 4-1 in Zagreb. When my alarm went off at 4am however all the doubts were gone. It was time, I was taking my own son to his first away game, a new era dawned and I was consumed by nostalgia.

Chapter 16
9732121- Bulgaria

"Where are your friends, mum?" Freddy asked as we sat on the plane waiting for boarding to complete. I laughed because this was typical. They had probably spent too much time in the pub and I now imagined them running through the airport swearing at each other to hurry up. I never had time to answer Freddy before I saw Perry's smirking face walking down the aisle.

I nodded at him and smiled but we had no time to catch up now as he was required to find his seat immediately. Me and Freddy chatted for a bit before he fell asleep. It was only 6am after all and we had a long day ahead of us. I wondered what the day and night would bring and what familiar faces I would stumble upon. I think I was as excited as Freddy to be honest. I had waited for what felt like a lifetime for this day to come. To finally be on a plane to an England away game again. Last time was Minsk 11 years ago and I was a completely different person back then. I hoped people would still find me fun to be around even when I wasn't swinging from the ceiling and punching the law enforcement.

After landing in Sofia we ended up far ahead of Perry and company in the passport queue and had to stand in the terminal waiting for them. Freddy didn't seem to mind at all, he was stood watching all the fans walking past. A parade of cheery football fans chatting and laughing. A few who I only knew by face nodded at me in recognition whereas others came over and started talking. Some really old faces from 2005 popped up and we had a catch up. They were all impressed by Freddy's presence.

"Only 9 and already at Bulgaria away eh kiddo? Not bad at all, I didn't even have a TV to watch football on at your age," laughed one of my friends who belonged to the older generation of football fans. I had known him and his wife since the early days and it was really good to see him still going strong and going football. I wanted that to be me in 20 years' time for sure.

"Mum you know everyone!" Freddy exclaimed after yet another group had called my name and came over to say hello. I laughed; I guess I had acquired quite a large circle of friends throughout the years and this airport wait was turning into somewhat of an meet and greet.

After circa 45 years, 76 familiar faces and 15 "Good to have you back", Perry and his posse finally joined us and after a quick chat we decided to take the metro to town. I had no clue what I was doing so I just followed Perry blindly. He was with his friend Paul and uncle Tony. It didn't take Freddy long at all to take a liking to them. I watched him as he was chatting to them about Birmingham City's season and as they were West Brom fans they had a bit of banter back and forth. Freddy had the gift of the gab for sure, and he was never short of a quick witty comeback much to the others bemusement.

"You wouldn't believe he's only 9, he seems so much older," said Perry as we walked out of the metro station.

"I know, its mad to think we were only a few years older than that when we first met at football eh," I replied and shivered at the thought of how quick time flies. I remember Geneva 05 with Perry and the others like it was yesterday. We were only teenagers and the world seemed so big.

Perry's hotel was at the other end of town so we decided to go check in and freshen up then meet back up later that evening.

Thanks to the modern phenomenon that is a certain map service on the phones we would be able to find our hotel easily. I put the address into the navigation system and it came up as a 29 minute walk.

I didn't tell Freddy we had that far to walk; it was sweltering hot and we were alone in what looked like the rougher parts of Sofia. There was no trouble in sight though and we had quite a pleasurable walk through the sunny town. Freddy stopped and posed for some photos and I finally got to upload his picture onto social media with the caption " Freddy's first away game."

The journey had truly began now. So had my sweating. I was soaked by the time we reached the hotel. We went up to our room and relaxed for a bit. My mother was delighted to receive a text informing her that everything was good and there was no drama for once. I could almost hear her grey hairs disappearing.

We got changed and got ready to go out into the afternoon and see what adventures awaited us. Freddy had not stopped smiling since we left and neither had I to be honest.

"Mum I absolutely love this," he said as we started walking down the strip. The city centre was one long strip filled with bars and cafes along both sides, and it was safe to say the English had taken over. Every bar had flags hung up outside and the clamouring of laughs and voices made a really nice background noise as we were walking in the afternoon sun. We never got far before we were stopped by some old a faces in an outdoor cafe. I introduced Freddy and they all seemed delighted to see that he had made it all the way over here to watch football with his mum. My old mate Jake, who's definitely not right in the head, popped up and started showing Freddy how many swipes he could do in a minute on a well-known dating app. Freddy just laughed as if to say " You're mad"

Few bars down we bumped into Gary, my old friend who I owed a drink since saving me from an arrest in Minsk. Me and Freddy went to the bar to get the drinks in. It was safe to say we made a very noticeable combo. There was no other young mum with her son present and it was an unusual sight at football over all. My hair was purple and bright as well so it was near impossible to miss us. Freddy seemed to love all the attention. Whilst I was queueing at the bar, he went to sit down on a bar stool by the wall. A big group of lads approached him instantly and he started chatting to them. They asked who he was here with and he pointed at me.

"Tell your sister to come over here mate, we will get your drinks in."

"That's not my sister that's my mum," laughed Freddy and waved me over. They got our drinks and we had a quick chat about where we were from and if this was his first game. Just like everyone else they seemed impressed by Freddy's presence. There was a lot of talk about the next generation. When we left them to take the drinks back Freddy was puzzled.

"I can't believe how friendly everyone is, it's like we all know each other"
"That's the point of it all mate. We're all family even if we haven't seen each other before," I replied as I balanced the drinks through the crowds to get back to Gary outside.

We sat with him for a while before Perry text us to say that they were in a lovely off street bar by their hotel. I looked it up and it was 30 minutes away. Freddy was really keen to go meet up with them and so we decided to take a stroll through Sofia. It really wasn't any bad atmosphere at this point and it was still light outside. Despite having already been up for 14 hours, Freddy showed no signs of being tired. He hadn't moaned once. I knew for sure that this wasn't going to be our last away game. I could tell from his enthusiasm that he had caught the bug that had no cure. The most contagious of them all. The football bug.

" No, no, show me again, I want to see the picture again." Freddy was laughing loud as Perry's uncle Tony yet again showed him a picture of when Perry dyed his hair blonde a few years back.
We were sat in the little backstreet bar they had met us in and we had ordered food. Freddy had looked at the menu a bit suspicious to start with and we all had slight doubts over what neck on cheese really was. We was having a right laugh together and I was amazed at how well my 9 year old son fitted into a group of mixed aged football fans. He looked like he had always been there.

The night continued as we made our way back onto the strip. Freddy had his own banter with the rest and I didn't even have to worry about him being bored. I had told him beforehand that this trip is all about him and what he wants. The second he's had enough of pubs we will call it a night. I had no plans on going on a wild bender this time.

We came across a smashed Villa fan and his apparent crazy mate from Liverpool. He spotted Freddy's Birmingham top and wanted to shake his hands. Freddy was a lad of principles however and so he refused to shake hand with someone supporting Villa. He wasn't rude but he made it perfectly clear that a handshake was not happening. Whilst the Liverpool lad was busy telling Tony and Paul about someone's head that got kicked in back in England, the Villa fan picked Freddy up. I could tell straight away that he didn't like it. His whole face changed. Perry saw it too and we quickly exchanged the familiar look that was telling each other that we might have to interfere here.
Luckily he put him back down and patted his back.

" You're a good lad despite supporting that shite blues," he slurred as he stumbled into the wall and onto his mate who was showing a video on his phone of said head kicking. He really was nothing but a harmless drunk man, but Freddy wasn't used to that.

"I didn't like him at all mum, and I didn't want to shake his hand," he whispered as we continued our walk to find a bar.

"Don't worry Freddy, we got Perry here who's ready to jump into your rescue any time," I laughed.

"I did think we would have to step in for a second there," admitted Perry and I agreed. The line between having a laugh and taking it too far is thin and he just about crossed it. We passed him a few more times that evening but he settled for shouting " Blues blues blues" at Freddy from a distance. Much to all our reliefs. Last thing we needed was a domestic brawl whilst in Bulgaria.

We sat in a bar down the strip for a while and soaked up the atmosphere. Freddy and Tony discussed the plot of the cult classic *Sharknado* and me and Perry were talking old memories. When you've known someone for as long as I had known Perry you sure have a lot of them in store. Geneva, Polish storming the pub in Manchester, Macedonia, Germany, Russia and so on. Paul was busy checking the local talent out on his dating app. It was around 9.30 when they got a call from their friend who was in another bar telling them to go there. It was significantly rowdier in that bar and indoors - it didn't feel like a place for a little 9 year old lad this time of the evening and so we decided to finish our drink and call it a night.

"See you tomorrow little man, get a good sleep now!" Tony said as he shook Freddy's hand when we left. We started walking down the strip. The sound of smashed bottles and chanting could be heard from all over the strip but it never felt at all hostile. It felt like familiarity to me if anything. We talked about our day the whole walk back and Freddy was ecstatic. He was going over the whole day and all the people and laughs we had.

"I can't wait for tomorrow, I really can't," he said as we walked up the stairs to our room. I couldn't either. Today had been nothing but perfect and I was overcome with gratitude to be back doing what I loved and to have my son by my side whilst doing it. When we got into bed my phone flashed. It was a notification telling me someone had tagged me in a photo on social media. I opened and there was a picture of me and Gary from earlier that day with the caption:
" Brilliant seeing this woman today – all those years ago following England together all over the globe; the drunkenness in Belarus , the war wounds in Russia - Welcome back Aza. Hope you and Freddy have a blast x"

I smiled and put my phone down. It was good to be back indeed.

"Its 9732121, don't forget that now," Freddy said to Lana. It was match day and we were sat in a bar in the sunshine along the strip. Freddy was busy telling people what taxi number was the only legit one and it had become somewhat of an in-joke throughout the day. We had been up early for hotel breakfast and walked to the shop for some snacks. We took a walk around the beautiful fountains and had a big pizza before meeting Lana and her friend Gem in the bar. Lana hadn't seen Freddy since he was a little baby and was amazed at the little lad he had grown into. He had them in stitches all day with his cheeky sense of humour. I got to take a back-seat for once and let Freddy take the driver seat. He sure knew how to keep people entertained. No one was missing me swinging from the ceiling I can assure you that much.

We stayed in the bar for a while before Perry texted us about meeting up. Lana knew of some roof top bar and we decided to go check it out. It was in this swanky hotel so we called them on our walk over there just to check if a 9 year old lad would be allowed in there and it was fine. We got a table overlooking Sofia and the lads soon joined us. They told us about Tony coming back at God knows what hour and throwing up everywhere. Freddy laughed; he really liked his banter with Tony and the fact he had spewed was not going to go unnoticed. We had already been and collected Lana's tickets and she had given them to us but the lads hadn't so we decided to come with them to collect. We said bye to Lana, who was flying home later. I had a string of pissed texts from Zeb but never managed to locate him. He called us when we were in the pub to ask for the number of the Freddy approved taxi and we all shouted "9732121" in unison.

When we got to the collection point the people looked at Freddy and asked if I had filled in a form required to get into the stadium. I gave Perry a puzzled look and the man hurried to clarify.

"As he's a minor you need to sign a weaver to say that you take full responsibility of him and anything that might happen to him, they won't let him into the stadium without one," he said as he slid me a document to fill in.

"Fucking hell, it's a good thing we came with you to collect tickets, otherwise we would've showed up to the ground and got turned away. Imagine my rage?" I muttered to Perry as we walked out of there. I had never heard of these before but I guess they wanted to have all bases covered.

"What is it about mum?" Freddy asked and looked at the document.

"Oh don't you worry, it's just a document to say that if you end up scrapping, your mums responsible," joked Tony and Freddy laughed.

"She's more likely to scrap than me to be fair," he replied and smiled at me. I laughed; the cheeky kid had definitely listened to one too many stories during this trip.

We had a beer in a pub by the collection point before making our way back down to the strip.
It was early evening now and the atmosphere was electric. Singing and chanting could be heard from all the pubs along the strip and a topless man was hanging out of a pub window as we walked past.

"Good on ye kid," he shouted at Freddy as we walked past. Freddy was beaming; he really had become somewhat of a mascot for the people during this trip and he loved being in the limelight.
We spent the rest of the time in the same bar and darkness was slowly settling in. Some Birmingham lads came up to Freddy and asked him to pose with them in front of their England and BCFC flag, something he gladly did. Time flew and it was time to head to the game. It was only a 30 min walk and everyone was walking in a steady stream down the main road so we decided to do the same.

The police presence were high and we had been warned about the hooligans from Bulgaria possibly jumping people on their walk to the stadium, but we saw nothing like that at all. It all seemed peaceful. When we got to the stadium they asked for the document; there was a short minute of confusion and I was asked to fill in yet another piece of paper. Freddy looked worried at this point as if he thought maybe this wouldn't go as planned after all and we wouldn't be able to watch the game. It was all formalities though and we were soon inside the Stadium.

All the England fans were squeezed into one corner of the stadium. It was predominately men and I saw no other children. Me and Freddy stuck out of the crowd like sore thumbs. Perry had ended up higher than us as we got separated but eventually managed to climb down to where we were. The atmosphere was intoxicating and as the singing started Freddy looked at me.

"I get what you mean with away games mum, I totally get what you mean." I squeezed his little hand and smiled back at him. The lads next to us was asking him what his teacher thought about him skipping school to go to football in Bulgaria.

"I didn't even lie, I just told him I was going here," he replied with a big smile.

The game kicked off and it became clear from the start that this was going to get nasty. The so called hooligans opposite us were stood with hoods up and doing Hitler salutes at us and monkey noises as soon as Sterling or any other player of colour had the ball. We had lost the game a few days earlier against Czech Republic so winning tonight was vital. Rashford scored after only 7 mins and the small section of England fans exploded in celebration. This spurred on the racists across the pitch even more and the taunting became unbearable. We started singing louder to drown them out and the sense of belonging had never been stronger. I thought about my dear father and how he would've showed me goosebumps on his arm at this point. Freddy didn't realise it until afterwards but he was experiencing a game that was to be talked about for a long, long time. Mings, who was making his England debut, was badly targeted and turned to us fans in despair when the monkey noises became unbearable. We sang our hearts out to lift him through it.

Barkley continued to add to Bulgaria's misery by scoring 0-2 around 20 minutes into the game.
All of a sudden the game was halted. A wave of confusion washed over everyone. Is this it?

Freddy looked at me and I had to explain what was going on. We were singing so loud to spur the lads on the pitch on that we could barely hear what the Bulgarians were doing but it was apparent that the lads on the pitch could and they now refused to play under such circumstances. My mum messaged me from home saying they were saying on TV that the game was to continue but would be stopped again if the racism wasn't controlled. Barkley scored 3-0 and it was looking good for us.

The chants from the hooded scum didn't stop however and just before half time the game was halted again. The players demanded a stop to this now. There is no room for racism in football, or anywhere else for that matter, and the players nor the fans would stand for this anymore. We continued to sing and try to lift the spirits. I was worried deep down that this was the end though and the game would be abandoned. I glanced at Freddy where he stood next to Perry chanting and wondered how much of this he really understood. All of a sudden a large group of the hooded hooligans were escorted out of the stand. The big screen showed how they all walked out whilst saluting Hitler and making noises.

"They've forced near 50 of the worst hooligans to leave, please be careful when you leave the stadium later, they're probably out there," Mum text me. I didn't show it to Freddy. This was his first England game and we were staying clear of any kind of trouble. Sterling scored just before half time making it a humiliating 0-4 to us. It was like we had been spurred on by the racism and wanted to prove to them that they couldn't break us.

" Who put the ball in the racist net? Raheem Fucking Sterling," we started singing, and Freddy looked at me as if to get permission to use the F word. I nodded at him. It was OK in this one circumstance for sure. He had never witnessed any racism before and this was a real eye opener for him. Watching him standing next to my mates singing proudly made me warm inside. The sense of belonging was bound to stay with him forever.

"Look here, we're on TV," the lad next to us said. The camera had zoomed in on all the fans singing when the game was halted and one of his friends back home had paused and took a picture of it to send him. He showed it us and there we were. In a big sea of big lads chanting you could see me and Freddy, both singing, both proudly. I gave the lad my number so that he could send me the picture. It'd be a dear memory for Freddy in years to come.

"It's a good thing you never lied to your teacher eh lad - he would of seen you on the TV thinking, he's not poorly, not one bit!" the lad next to us laughed.

Second half was nothing but a triumph. The lads on the pitch stood tall and the fans sang loud. Sterling scored again and Kane finally made it a victorious 0-6 win to England on a night none of us would forget anytime soon. When the whistle blew we all celebrated and continued to sing long after the game had finished. The players walked up to us and thanked us by clapping and we saluted them. The mutual love between players and fans were unyielding right now.

"What a first game for you to be at," said the man next to us as we were queuing to leave the poignant stadium behind us.

"It's not my last," Freddy replied and winked at me in the absolute cheekiest way possible.

When we got out of the stadium there was police everywhere. Big vans were lining up along the whole main road and it became clear that we would not be attacked. Despite whispers about the ultras waiting for us there wasn't a hint of brawl during the walk. I've been there before; I know when an atmosphere is hostile and this wasn't it. There was no tension as we made our way home through the warm October night. I looked at Freddy where he was walking next to Paul and Perry chatting to them about his impressions of the night we had. I could almost see myself, 15 years ago, walking back from the pub with my dad after my first away game. All the dreams and hopes I had that night, the feeling of knowing that it was the start of something big. People used to laugh at me when I was 14 and told them I would live in England one day and go to football all the time. Good thing I never listened to anyone else eh?

I couldn't put a price on the 15 years of memories football had given me. The laughs, the tears and the triumph. The unwavering love I felt for football had not faded, it had grew stronger. Russia was no longer nothing but a distant blip amongst a massive collection of good times with good people. These people I had met the past decade were friends I knew I would have for life. We would watch each other's children grow up and follow in our footsteps. Generations would shift but the pride of following your football wouldn't. I wondered if Freddy would walk down a street one night with his son or daughter after an away game and think about this night and how it all began here, a warm October evening in Sofia after a game that got halted twice due to racism. Would he fondly spend hours telling his own children about how him and his mum spent his childhood travelling to different countries to watch football? Would tonight be the start of his very own story?

I glanced down on my arm, the tattoo was still there. It was now surrounded by a full sleeve but never did I regret it. It was on my skin just as it was in my heart. Forever England. We got to the food place and as it was late it was time for me and Freddy to head back to the hotel. The food Perry was in the process of ordering looked highly questionable and I didn't want to be around for when his body realised it's grave mistake. We said bye and as we started walking away Freddy turned around.

"9732121, don't forget that when you're taking the taxi to the airport!"
I could hear their laughs echo through the warm Bulgarian night.

Chapter 17
Unsuccessful in ballot

"Have you heard the news?" My mate sent me a message but he didn't have to. It was impossible not to have heard the news. It was 6 months after the glorious trip to Bulgaria. Me, Freddy and my dear father had started planning for the 2020 Euros. We had tickets for both 2 of the group games and the semi-final at Wembley. The idea of experiencing a tournament at Wembley with my dad and son was making my whole body jitter with excitement. Well at least up until today, Tuesday the 17th of March 2020. I was sat in my car waiting for Mia and Freddy to come out of school when I got the news. The virus that had emerged the past month and had been declared a pandemic had now claimed another victim. The Euros.

As you can imagine I didn't take the news very well. I had kept a brave face on the past month whilst watching the world fall apart - but I couldn't anymore. I know it might sound trivial in a situation where people are dying daily from the virus, but for me and so many like me, football was a lifeline.

It had offered a sense of normality, and now that it was declared that there will be no Premier league or Euros it all felt surreal. I really struggled the upcoming months but kept a brave face on for the sake of the children. I had been in a relationship with someone new called Jack for 5 months. Jack was everything I had always been missing. Supportive, funny, and absolutely forgiving when it came to my football outbursts and general silliness. He supported Aston Villa and the fact we both loved football was something that instantly bonded us. Due to the new lockdown rules we weren't allowed to see each other. Needless to say it was a dire chapter of our lives. I feel like the pandemic has claimed enough of peoples time and sanity - no one needs to read any more about it.

We were all told that the Euros would be postponed to June 2021 and that our tickets would be valid then. That was over a year from now and this whole thing would be blown over by then…

Let's fast forward a year ahead and enjoy the fact that we are now pandemic free and sport is back on and… oh wait. The pandemic is still going! Unless you're reading this book 100s of years from now you already knew that, though. By this time we had sort of gotten used to it however. Premier League was back on and things were half back to normal, but second and third variants of the virus kept rearing their ugly heads. In the last 12 months my kids had been in school around half of the year - the rest was home-schooling, and most people now worked from home permanently. It was a new world but somehow we adapted. It wasn't until I found out that the Euros would be going through with reduced capacity that I once again lost my mind a bit. I didn't know if I had tickets or not anymore.

Weeks of uncertainty and rumours followed. I had just gotten in from work and started preparing dinner when I received an email. With hands full of parsley all over them I opened the email.

"Unsuccessful in ballot." My heart sank. I guess I had held on to the hope of keeping my tickets but it was now confirmed. Freddy and I had lost all 3 tickets each and could expect a refund of £1300 soon. Never had that amount of money tasted worse. I spent it on trainers but not even they could help me run away from the fact I lost the tickets.

I became a bit of a bitter nightmare the next few weeks. Soon as someone mentioned the Euros I met it with a sigh. I can be really dramatic like that. My dad declared he wasn't even going to watch it - he had also lost all his tickets. It wasn't until someone asked Freddy if he was excited about the Euros and he just shrugged his shoulders that I realised that my own bitterness had killed his enthusiasm. I didn't like the idea of that, so I went and got him an England top, a Euro wall chart and the Panini sticker book. The Euro feeling started to land in the household. I didn't feel it though. Knowing we should be going to England-Croatia on the Sunday but had to watch it on TV was just too much of a hard pill to swallow. It wasn't until I sat down that Friday night to watch the opening ceremony with Jack, my other half, that I felt it for the first time. It was Italy-Turkey, and when Bocelli sang *Nessun Dorma* the hair on my arms stood up. The Euro feeling had finally got me.

It's funny how you tell yourself you're not going to bother with something but get struck down last minute. I guess you can't fight deep rooted love eh?

I'm glad I decided to get involved because the weeks that followed will go down as some of the best weeks of my life.

Chapter 18

Germany are crying

" Jack!! Look here, look what it says!" I was jumping up and down next to Jack, who had been standing talking to our friend Will. It was a warm Saturday evening in June, a couple of weeks into the Euros. We were at a friend's leaving party and I had been complaining that we must make it back for the 8PM kick off that evening. You see, when the Euros or the World Cup starts that's all I'm breathing and living for a month. Everything else becomes unwanted background noise, and despite losing all our tickets I was once again fully wrapped up in this tournament.

We had finished the group stage with a 1-0 win against Croatia, a 0-0 draw against Scotland that we'd rather not mention and another 1-0 win over the Czechs. Sterling had scored both goals. Was it overly impressive? Perhaps not - but we were making history by not conceding any goals. Pickford was having the tournament of his life and Southgate's tactics seemed to work. The next game that awaited was round of 16 against.. wait for it.. the Germans! And that takes us directly back to this warm Saturday evening in a pub garden where I was now jumping up and down waving my phone in Jack's face.

" What's up babe?" he laughed. He wasn't used to me being this enthusiastic at social events.

" I've got an email from the FA saying I'm successful in the ballot for a ticket against Germany!"

" You're joking? That's fantastic news!"

He proceeded to tell Will all about my ticket heartache and how many times UEFA had emailed me in the past two weeks about being unsuccessful in yet another ballots, ballots I didn't even know

I was in. They just loved writing emails about one's unsuccessful status I guess. I was lost in utter glee for a bit, waving my phone in people's faces repeatedly. It wasn't until I read further down in my email that I realised I had acted hastily and that I was in fact not guaranteed a ticket. I would be sent an exclusive access code the following morning at 10am and it would then be my responsibility to try and buy a ticket before they got snapped up by the rest of the successful applicants. This was usually within minutes.

My excitement soon shifted onto stress. I had a chance to get a ticket and I be damned if I messed this up. Freddy was unsuccessful but was away on his residential leaver's trip anyway, so I decided it would be ok to go without him for once. I didn't relax for the rest of the evening. Poor Jack had to put up with my endless "what if I mess this up and miss out?" speeches. What if I did though? I had completely written off going to the Euros and had accepted that it would be followed on a screen but now they were dangling this carrot in front of me I instantly knew that I had to go. I spent the night tossing and turning whilst thinking about songs that mentions the war…

The following morning I was up early. I was a bit frazzled if I'm honest. My phone which was from the stone-age just glitched whenever I logged into the ticket portal and I could feel the tickets slipping away. Perry text me just before to remind me and I ended up having to send my access code to him and my log in to buy the ticket as my phone wasn't feeling very cooperative. He told me to leave it with him and so I did. The sale started 10am and I think it was 10.02 when he text me to say he got me one. I was going to watch England – Germany in a knock out stage at Wembley.
My mouth was watering just at the idea. I think poor Jack had to put up with me talking about absolutely nothing else for the next few days whilst leaving a trail of saliva after me wherever I went.

" It's one in, one out," declared the large and loud security guard outside the fan park at Wembley.

It was around 1pm and I had come down alone on the train to Wembley. I had been nervous all day and it wasn't letting go. I was meeting Perry, Paul and Tony who Freddy and I had spent Bulgaria with. They were inside the fan park at a table and texted me to just let the security know that, but they were having none of it. Others thought that I was trying to push the queue and told me that this isn't a pick up scene. I laughed to myself. If you're a girl at football you obviously must be there for the men. No offence but the idea that one would struggle so immensely to pick up men that they joined a football club and paid to travel the world just to meet them was humorous. A steady formation and passing in triangle form was much more of a turn on for me than anything else. Perry had appeared in the doorway now and was chatting to the security guard. I was called over and instantly let in.

There was a wave of muttering and booing as I was let in ahead of everyone else, and as the awkwardly polite person I am I was uttering "sorry" a thousand times as I squeezed past walls of sweaty angry bodies who had probably stood in this queue for hours. By the looks of things they would still be in this queue after full time.

The atmosphere inside was fantastic. I hadn't seen the lads since Bulgaria so we had a lot to catch up on - but you don't really do that in the lead up to a game. You sing, drink and the only words you keep exchanging between each other are " fuck I'm nervous now are you?" or " what drink do you want?"

It's quite a beautiful thing. The art of bonding with people without having to engage in deep conversations. You are all there for the same reason and that's enough.

" Germany's gone 7 games unbeaten so far you know," said one of the lads in the group as we zigged zagged past people down Wembley way towards the stadium.

It was hard not to think of past heartache when you thought about England- Germany. Our gaffer Southgate himself knew all about that after his penalty pain 96. Could things change tonight?

It sure felt like it could. Wembley felt electric the second we stepped inside. I was stood on my own so made my way over to my spot behind goal. I have no problem going on my own because you're never alone at football. For the next few hours the people around you are your friends. You share happiness and sorrow. You hug, you kiss and you swear. Or judging by the man next to me, you sweat profusely.

" Fucking hell I've got the evening sun straight in my eyes," he said as he wiped his forehead with the back of his hand. He had a broad northern accent and was flicking through the match programme. I hadn't bothered getting one because I'm a little superstitious when it comes to sport and I had never bought one previously. Silly I know, but some pre game rituals just had to stay the same. I carried Freddy's lucky penny in my pocket every time England played. It was made 1966 and that in itself felt like a strange coincidence. It was roughly 10 mins until kick off and the nerves had truly kicked in. I had joined the man next to me in the sweating and I had that immensely strange feeling in my stomach. I was here now. There was nothing else in this moment. Just 90 mins of uncertainty and gut wrenching anxiety. It was time for the national anthem and as the first line echoed out over the 45,000 something fans at Wembley, I felt a familiar wave of pride and love wash over me. This was it.

After a few minutes it seemed like Germany had took a grip of the game. We struggled to break through despite several free kicks. Kane just couldn't find himself. I think he had 2-3 touches in the first half. It was a bit frustrating to watch but something we were used to. Pickford was dishing up save after save but it felt like we would run out of luck eventually if we didn't offer anything on the offensive side of things.

" I don't get what's up with Kane this tournament, he better shape the fuck up," said the lad next to me. I don't know if he was talking to me or in general but I nodded in agreement. I had hoped we'd be in the lead by now so we could relax a bit. This rollercoaster of a half was messing with my inner peace to say the least. I don't think I could hack the Germans knocking us out at Wembley.

Second half kicked off and Germany instantly had a chance again which was denied by Pickford. Couldn't love him more than I did right then.

Jack Grealish was seen on the screen warming up and fans immediately started chanting for him.

Could he be the change we needed? The game were heading towards the later stage of the half and still 0-0. I told myself that if it came to penalties against Germany I would leave. I probably wouldn't if it really came to it but it's just one of them things I tell myself when football gets tense. It' s comforting to tell yourself you have the choice at least I guess.

A few minutes later Sterling passes Kane who shuttles it to Grealish. Jack to Shaw and the low cross into the box is tapped in by Sterling.

And Wembley erupts. People are jumping over us from the rows behind and despite being sent straight into the chair in front of me I'm delirious with happiness. You just can't beat that feeling. You can try but I promise you can't. It's like a drug I will forever chase the high of.

It took a good few minutes to settle back down to earth and try catch our breathes but we didn't get to remain calm for long as Muller comes free. Thousand thoughts went through my head as he prepares to shoot but it goes wide and the whole of Wembley can breathe out.

" I need a defibrillator after this," I said to the lad next to me who laughed and agreed, face still gleaming with sweat.

Around 10 minutes later and in the very last few minutes of the game Shaw wins the ball from the German midfield and Kane seems to finally stand in the right spot to send England into the quarter final whilst also sending Germany home. Absolute scenes followed and most of us lost both voice and sense. Germany cried on the big screen and Joachim Low sniffed his hands for one last time.

They smelt of everything but victory that's for sure.

I stayed for a while singing and chanting before realising that I had a train to catch. I had work the next morning and could not afford some re-run of my past of missing trains right left and centre.

I smiled as I walked down the road from Wembley. It was full of people celebrating, drinking and laughing. It was the best sound in the world. It was slowly fading behind me as I went down to the train station. Something that wouldn't fade was the memory of this evening.

I couldn't believe that after a year of pandemic and misery I was walking back from Wembley after seeing England knock Germany out. It felt surreal. Like the past year had never happened.

I was at football again. In the end, that was all I needed to feel hope.

Chapter 19

Semi-final – Good times never seemed so good

"I can't believe it mum, I really can't!" Freddy's face was beaming when I told him I had got us tickets for England's semi-final at Wembley. It was a week after the game against Germany and we had since then slaughtered Ukraine in the quarter final and was now facing Denmark in a semi -final played at Wembley. This tournament had gone from something I was bitter about to an absolute dream. I was so wrapped up in the Euros that I probably would have lost my job if it wasn't for the fact I was the manager. When I was younger my mum used to call school and tell them I was sick when in fact I was at football or watching football on tv. I even pulled a sickie once to watch a draw for the Euros. The worst excuse I ever used was when I told my driving instructor that I couldn't do my lesson due to a family tragedy. The tragedy was that Luton manager Nathan Jones had gone to Stoke.

Freddy and I booked ourselves a shithole of a hotel by Wembley just for the authenticity of it. It's not a proper England game unless you get to stumble out of some questionable accommodation whilst swearing over how you may as well sleep on the floor the mattress is that hard.

Our experience was just like that. 6th floor and the lift wasn't working. Freddy took the steps seemingly well but it was a different story for me. I was huffing and puffing behind him like a chain smoking 80 year old doing body pump. The whole hotel screamed eastern European shithole and our room had a weird clicking noise inside of it. We decided the less time spent inside this room the better and instantly set off out. Perry was texting us to hurry up as he once again had a table in the fan park but had been told if we didn't get there soon they would give our spots up.

As we arrived to the fan park we was met by a security guard who had recently received his PHD in people skills. When we tried to explain to him that we had spots at a table inside he picked up his megaphone and shouted in our faces

" We are at full capacity."

"Yeah ok mate no need to shout in my sons face is there?" I snapped at him whilst imagining taking his stupid megaphone and whack him with it. I don't do football violence anymore though, so I quickly let go of that idea, however appealing. I texted Perry to tell him the security was having a hissy and he soon appeared in the door, chatting to the female security guard who called us over to be let in. I walked past the angry security guard with a smug look.

" Come here kidda, I haven't seen you for years!" Tony exclaimed, and embraced Freddy. It was two years since we had spent Bulgaria with them and Freddy had become somewhat of a legend back then. Tony had his phone out to show Freddy a picture he still had of him in Bulgaria with some blues fans. The atmosphere inside was absolutely rocking and Freddy was soon stood on a chair singing freed from desire. The security guard told him to get off his chair however. You got to watch it with these little hooligan kids aren't you. You never know what sort of uproar they're going to cause. Especially not 11 year old little kids high on sugar and life, massive security threat when they stand on chairs…

Despite security doing their utmost to ruin the fun and atmosphere we had a cracking afternoon. It was easy to forget we had a massive game ahead of us. It's like that sometimes. You get so caught up in the pre-game euphoria and then it hits you all of a sudden: we have a massive game in an hour. The nerves kick in and you become absolutely useless socially. Freddy had been gone for about 20 minutes and I was looking around the big hall wondering where he was. Had security finally obtained him and identified him as a potential threat to fan-park security? Football legend Rio Ferdinand made an appearance and sang a few songs with the fans whilst making his way up the stairs. Freddy appeared shortly after whilst waving his phone in my face.

" Where have you been? I was about to have your name called out on the speaker," I joked.

" You will never believe who I met," he answered, and got a photo up on his phone of him and Mo Farrah chilling together. I laughed. This was typical Freddy. Absolutely no qualms about chasing Mo Farrah down for a photo. Mo can outrun most people but not Freddy it seemed.

We made our way to Wembley shortly after. Wembley way was packed to its brim and we could barely move forward but we got there in the end. We stopped at the top of the stairs just before the entrance.

"Turn around Freddy and take that in."

Freddy turned around and behind us was a never-ending sea of people all making their way to Wembley. All full of the same excitement and nerves as we were. There was no end to the stream of people. It felt infinite. We continued into the stadium and as we took the last familiar steps and Wembley opened up before us I took a deep breath.

" Fucking hell can you feel that atmosphere already?"

It felt familiar but so different. We had been here so many times but tonight felt different. I can't quite explain it - it felt magic. The evening sun was shimmering over the grass and as it was being watered down it created little rainbows inside the streams of water.

I felt my heart beating in my chest. A semi- final at Wembley. This was the stuff I used to dream about when I was younger. To be stood here one day and watch us go into a final. Was that dream about to come true here tonight? It felt like it. It really did.

"Azaaaa!!" I turned around and through the masses of people came my old mate from the early England days, Neil. Me and dad used to meet up with him before the games and seeing his excited face made nothing but fond memories come flooding back. We got lost in nostalgia for a bit and we told Freddy about some of the old memories we've shared. You know you've reached a certain age when you can look at you children and say: "back when we were young and going football.."

The crowd started up Southgate you're the one at such a volume I couldn't hear my beating heart anymore. The man in front of us turned around to us with tears in his eyes. He had a look of complete and utter overwhelm on his face and I think we all felt it. It might sound silly but it was one of those moments that you knew would stay with you forever.

" I'm nervous now, mum." Freddy looked at me whilst fidgeting with his water bottle. I felt the same. I squeezed his shoulder as the team lined up to sing the national anthem.

" This is it son, this is it."

"I can't stand that Danish clown – he's nowhere near the man his father was," I muttered to Freddy as Schmeichel denied us goal after goal. He had made some rather cocky comments before the game and I felt my dislike for his smug face grow like a fireball in my stomach. It had been a frustrating first 25. We just couldn't seem to break them down. I was getting increasingly frustrated and when Denmark scored 1-0 on a freekick around the 30 min mark I felt my foot kick the chair in front of me with such force it left a mark on my immaculate trainers. I sunk down in my seat for a moment. Me and Freddy didn't say anything to each other. What was there to say?

Football is such a harsh contrast between heaven and hell. You slip between both of them for 90 minutes and there is just no way of telling where you'll eventually land.

We looked rattled after the goal. All over the place, much like my intense mood swings.

10 minutes of unsettled play followed and I was begging they wouldn't cement a 2-0 lead before half time. Nor my nerves or my trainers could handle that.

All of a sudden Kane finds Saka with a mighty fine pass, Sterling is set to tuck it in but Denmark's Kjaer beat him to it, and its 1-1 just 5 minutes before half time.

The helter-skelter of ups and downs took us to the absolute top and we erupted in a big sweaty mess of jumping on top of each other. Wembley was once again rocking and the little hairs on my arm stood up as if to greet this feeling of euphoria.

Half time was spent catching our breathe. Freddy was chatting to the lads next to us. He had a fantastic ability to make friends wherever we went. His astute match analysis and sharp witty banter always seemed to have people taking an instant liking to him. The man in-front of us went and got Freddy a bottle of water at half time after Freddy had mentioned being absolutely parched. It was gestures like that which made the football such a special community. It was only a bottle of water but it signified something much bigger, something we all felt that evening. An intense sense of belonging and comradeship. Second half kicked off and we all belted out god save the queen as always.

Second half was a nervy story. As expected, Denmark was not going down without a fight and we seemed to go through every range of emotion there was. I took a sip of Freddy's water and gathered myself. I glanced over at Freddy where he was stood. His little hands were squeezing the lucky penny and his eyes were focused on the events on the pitch. When the final whistle blew and it became clear that we once again were going into extra time in an important game I felt like crying.

I don't know why but these things never seemed to end well for us and some premature crying might not have been the worst idea but I held it back. Someone once described me as: "that Swedish bird who always cry at the football." I think it was meant as an insult but there was absolutely no lie in it. I was a sobby mess when I watched football. I don't know why but I just seemed to become overwhelmed with emotions. Had been that way since I was a child and cried after England got knocked out against Argentina. I was determined the only tears I be crying tonight were those of joy however.

"I am so nervous I don't know where to turn," said Freddy with a mix of excitement and fear, and his newfound friends next to him agreed. They patted him on the back as the extra time kicked off.

Schmeichel almost instantly denied Kane a goal and my fists were clenched along with my jaws. I felt so tense and the next 10 minutes is a bit of a blur. We were singing so loud to push the lads on that I think I burst some blood vessels for sure. Then Kane goes down in the penalty area.

A wave of people gasping went through Wembley. They were doing a VAR check and I didn't even dare to look at Freddy at this point.

" It's a penalty!" he shouts and I grabbed his hand. Kane steps up and for a split second my world stopped. There was just Kane and the ball. All noise went away. He takes the shot and.. he misses it…

I was just about to have break down of the century when there's an instant rebound and Kane goes and fucking scores. I'm going to say that again just for added effect.

Kane went and fucking scored the rebound on extra time in the semi-final.

I'm not even going to try and put the emotions that followed into words. It's not possible. You had to be there. It was such a powerful explosion that I lost all sense of reality celebrating.

When I turned around to Freddy he had his top off, waving it in the air.

The lads next to him follow suit and as they've all stripped off they pick him up in the air.

The time left of extra time that followed was just one big celebration. It seemed as if we had forgotten that Denmark still could score and force us to partake in penalties, something we're not the best at. They didn't though. They had no energy left in them to reply to our 2-1 goal. When the final whistle blew we all knew that what we were witnessing was history. England had never been in a Euro final before, and most of us certainly had never experienced us winning any trophies.

Drinks were flying in the air as the crowd started to belt out *Sweet Caroline*. Neil comes charging in from nowhere and join us in singing. Freddy was standing on his chair topless and with a look on his face I've never seen before: possibly his first moment of football euphoria. I took it all in. Wembley in- front of me in all its glory. The players in a pile on the floor celebrating. The fans embracing each other screaming the lyrics to *Sweet Caroline* and Freddy in the middle of it all.

This.

This is what we live for. This feeling of utter and uncomplicated love.

I wanted to bottle this feeling and have it injected into my veins forever.

Good times never seemed so good. So good.

Chapter 20 – The final

"I just can't wrap my head around it – we're in the final" I said to Jack as we took Mia ice skating the day before. He was demolishing a cheese and onion pasty and nodded in agreement.

I needed some sort of detachment from the fact the final was tomorrow, so we had a whole day out with Mia. Freddy was playing Gaelic. I had been run down and drained since we got back from the semi-final and my health couldn't wait for the Euros to be over so I could recover. My heart didn't want it to be over though. I would gladly live in this vacuum of football exhaustion forever. England would be playing Italy in the final - we missed out on tickets by one cap. I couldn't argue with that logic. Tickets to a final should go to those who had been the most games and we had only done Bulgaria away and a few home games in the previous campaign. Part of me was gutted, but the other part was OK with it. I don't know if my fragile health could take a final at Wembley. My tendencies towards violence had to be kept under control and I'm not sure they would if we were there and lost. When you're 35 you tend to know and respect where your personal limitation lies. Me, Jack and Freddy booked a table at the local pub, along with Jack's mate George. It was a 8pm kick off and I knew already now that all Sunday would be spent stuck in a mental panic room unable to escape.

" I don't know if it was the vindaloo or nerves but my god my stomach is in bits," I announced to Freddy as we were getting ready to drop Mia at her dad's before the pub. He looked at me where I was stood in the hall rubbing my gut.

" Don't be disgusting mum, no one needs to know that," he declared - and I suppose he was right.

The fact still remained though that my body was on complete and utter shutdown. The nerves had taken over and my drive over to their dad was slightly erratic. Mia was mildly upset that she wasn't coming the pub with us but I just couldn't bear to bring her to what could be a quite hostile atmosphere. I trusted Freddy to remain calm if things kicked off, but I couldn't subject my 8 year old daughter to anything like that.

" I really hope they win for you mum," she said as we hugged goodbye.

I hope so too, I thought to myself as I walked back to the car. Me and Freddy didn't say much on the drive over to Jack's. We were staying there for the night so we could just walk back afterwards.

Afterwards. The whole idea of afterwards were scary at this moment. It could either be a night of endless celebrating, jumping into fountains or jumping on tables, or it could end in utter heartache, again. When we arrived at Jack's the atmosphere were tense. We didn't know what to do with ourselves. We just sat in the lounge staring at each other until Jack eventually stood up.

" Nah shall we just go? I can't wait any longer."

Neither could I. As we left the house I looked at Freddy and Jack.

" This could be the last time we lock the door without having won the Euros," I said and gave them another eerie look. They sighed.

" Please don't jinx it mum, you've said that about absolutely everything we've done today," Freddy complained. Jack laughed and I just shrugged my shoulders.

" Nothing wrong with dreaming, son. Nothing wrong with dreaming."

" Do you think 55 years of hurt ends tonight?" I asked Freddy as we tucked into our pre game food down the pub.

" I hope so," he answered but he didn't sound too hopeful. Italy had been really strong so far in the tournament but so had we. 1 goal conceded in a whole tournament. First final in 55 years. History was unfolding right in-front of our eyes and it was easy to get dragged into the belief that this was in fact the summer when football came home. We had been in a pandemic for over a year now and people needed something to hang on to. A little bit of hope in a dark world. These players had given us just that. A whole nation had forgot about social distancing and vaccines for four weeks and united in their love for football. It had been wonderful to see and to be a part of and regardless of tonight's result I do believe that on some level, football was already home.

We spent the hour before the game singing and banging the tables. We hadn't watched any of the games in the pub so far and this was an experience in itself. It wasn't Wembley but it would do for us. We were together and in two hours we would hopefully be all over each other on the floor celebrating. The game was kicking off and I stood up to sing the anthem. It don't matter if I'm at the game or not, I will stand up and sing the anthem.

I nodded at Freddy as the whistle blew and he nodded back. Words felt excessive right now.

You're watching your team in a final. There's no words for that.

" Oh my fucking god I can't believe it!" I howled at Freddy and Jack as Luke Shaw went and scored 1-0 for us after only 1 minute and 57 seconds. Was this happening? I think on some level beforehand I had sort of expected us to lose in the final. It was the sort of heartache we were used to but watching us bang in a goal the first 2 minutes woke hope in me I didn't even know was there. I was on cloud nine celebrating and all I could say was: " We're doing it, were fucking doing it!!!" again and again. Freddy was embracing the others and it took a while before we landed back down to an acceptable functional level. In my head I was thinking about the night ahead. About the songs and about Freddy dancing on tables. I imagined us showing up late the following day to school still wearing football tops and absolutely delirious. I allowed my mind to go there. It's a dangerous place but fuck it's nice to visit now and then.

We kept them off us first half, and at half time I was that exhausted I went outside for a smoke. I'm not a smoker as such but when I'm nervous at football I've been known to chain-smoke.

" You know what? I think we got this," Jack said as we were stood outside in the smoking area, hiding from the downpour.

" Me too," I admitted whilst blowing out the smoke slowly. We exchanged what I think was a look of hope before we went back inside.

Italy had the pressure in second half and I felt more and more nervous. There was times where I was turning away from the scree, in pure terror. I didn't know if we could hold them back for another 20 mins.

I soon got my answer to that musing when the mega ancient Bunocci tapped it in and making it 1-1.

The whole pub went silent and you could almost hear peoples hopes slowly fading away. We had started so strong with that early goal and then spent most of the game fighting to keep it 1-0 and now we had given it away with 20 odd minutes left it all felt like a bad dream. I didn't say a word. Didn't look at anyone. Just sat silently on my chair staring into the abyss. Freddy was doing the same. Jack went for a smoke. George sighed and went the bar. The game went into extra time and I still couldn't bring myself to say anything. As the clock ticked on I was filled with fear. Not penalties. Anything but an outcome determined by penalties. When the whistle blew and it became clear that our fate indeed would be determined by penalties I felt tears burning behind my eyes. We couldn't lose this. Not like this.

" I don't know if I can take this," I mumbled to the rest who all looked on in despair.

We stood up around the table. My hands were firmly squeezing the chair in-front of me. Freddy looked teary. Jacks appeared back from yet another stress smoke and George was wiping his forehead. There was so much emotion in play that moment it's hard to even re-tell.

Please please please I thought to myself. The pub was silent. There was no singing at this point. There was just the penalty shoot-out.

Italy went first with Berardi and scored. I swore to myself. Kane followed by scoring as well and for a split second we got to celebrate again. It's weird when you celebrate during a penalty shoot-out. You sort of celebrate but in a more subdued way as you know it is far from over at that point.

Belotti takes the next penalty and Pickford saves it. Celebration again and a small glimmer of hope. This was cemented further when Maguire score for us. We now had the grip of this shoot-out. Once again I allowed myself to dream. It was only a short dream but images of a wild nights celebration flashed before my eyes briefly. Could we actually be winning this final on penalties? My whole body was jittery and anxious. So close. So so close now. Italy's Bonucci scored theirs and things intensified further. Rashford steps up. It felt safe. I've watched this man score penalties for United in his sleep.

He missed it.

He fucking missed it. I started to sink down in my chair as Italy went and scored 3-2. I knew this.

Everyone knew this. We had lived this before. Southgate had lived this before. I glanced up just as Sancho missed his. Freddy were standing up with his hands on his head. Not a word was said. Jack and George were doing the same. Italy went and missed theirs, there wasn't much of a celebration as people were too nervy. Saka has to score this one now or it would be over.

I once again stood up, heart exploding in my chest, eyes fixated on the screen where Saka stood in-front of the ball. It felt like the whole of England held their breath as he stepped up and…

Missed it. The silence was so loud it was numbing. The images on the screen of the Italians celebrating whilst we sunk to the bottom. I felt the tears streaming down my cheeks. I angrily wiped them off. I didn't want to cry right now but the emotions did what they wanted to it seemed.

Freddy was crying too and I felt like I needed to get him out of here. Away from this horrible evening. His first real football heartbreak. The first of many. I nodded at the others and started to lead a sobbing Freddy through the crowd of disappointment. There was a few sympathetic looks and pats on his back as we passed people. Outside I embraced him and tried to put on a brave face but I was teary too. We had lived this dream for a month

" It wasn't our time mate, it wasn't our time," I whispered as his sobbing continued.

Jack appeared from the toilet and we walked home. It seemed a different walk now than the one we did earlier. We were filled with hope then and now it was just numbness. Jack was ranting whilst me and Freddy just walked in silence. To be so close but still fall on the very last hurdle.

When we got in Freddy instantly went up to bed. I went in to chat to him a little bit before he went to sleep.

He was tucked up in bed. His little face sticking out from the quilt and still tears in his eyes.

"We have had the best summer, mate, we really have. This isn't the end – it's just the beginning. We have a really young squad and every tournament we get one step closer to that trophy"

"It's just so cruel," he sighed as he sunk further and further into the bed.

I felt a wave of familiarity wash over me. We had been here before. 23 years ago to be precise.

A parent had sat on the edge of their child's bed trying to console them after England had lost.

I knew there was only one thing left to say. One thing that had stayed with me my whole life, which had echoed in my head every-time we lost a game. I felt the circle closing, a whole life of football memories briefly flashed before my eyes. I could almost hear my dad's voice as I said it.

"There will come a day tomorrow again, when the grass will still be green, the sky blue and the house will still be here. Things will go on."

Printed in Great Britain
by Amazon

19692922R00088